What people are say

A Reason to Carry On

Right from the start of the book I was impressed by how knowledgeable the author was in the workings of the human psyche. Her journey towards understanding the meaning of life brought her close to a multitude of individuals who had gone through grief and adverse conditions. Yvonne's dedication to them, as a physical therapist with in-depth knowledge of psychology, not only helped a great many of them overcome their difficulties but also gave her a deep appreciation of how these particular individuals got to that specific point in their lives and how they coped, or not, with their problems.

The author's life being full of strange almost metaphysical coincidences has served her well in her quest for the meaning of life. Admirable.

Doreen Wells, Marchioness of Londonderry

A Reason to Carry On

The meaning of life is within
each of us to grasp

A Reason
to Carry On

The meaning of life is within
each of us to grasp

Vony Eichel

**PSYCHE
BOOKS**

Winchester, UK
Washington, USA

JOHN HUNT PUBLISHING

First published by Psyche Books, 2022
Psyche Books is an imprint of John Hunt Publishing Ltd., No. 3 East St., Alresford,
Hampshire SO24 9EE, UK
office@jhpbooks.com
www.johnhuntpublishing.com
www.psyche-books.com

For distributor details and how to order please visit the 'Ordering' section on our website.

Text copyright: Vony Eichel 2021

ISBN: 978 1 80341 014 2
978 1 80341 015 9 (ebook)
Library of Congress Control Number: 2021915400

A CIP catalogue record for this book is available from the British Library.

Design: Stuart Davies

UK: Printed and bound by CPI Group (UK) Ltd, Croydon, CR0 4YY
Printed in North America by CPI GPS partners

We operate a distinctive and ethical publishing philosophy in
all areas of our business, from our global network of authors to
production and worldwide distribution.

Contents

For Nathalie, Annabelle, Bruce, James and Benjamin

Preface

Many people journey through life failing to discover a reason or purpose for their existence. Some are satisfied, through procreation, to have fulfilled their duty, through the continuity of their gene pool. Others identify themselves through their offspring, whilst others through their career. Then there are those, who in spite or lack of a contribution to society, question and ponder what it was all for. True fulfillment lies in finding real meaning in life. This book is designed for people at all stages of life to contemplate further what life is about, as well as those looking for a reason to carry on.

I want to thank all my wonderful teachers, friends and students who inspired me. Thank you to Coral Temple for her support.

A special big thanks to Julius Melnitzer, of Toronto, Canada, who wholeheartedly gave so much of his valuable time and energy into shaping the final copy.

What I am about to share with you is an accurate rendition of events to the best of my ability. Naturally, for reasons of confidentiality, I have changed all the names, as well as any details that might reveal the actual persons involved. Still, the key events are undeniable.

Introduction

Thou sustainest the living with loving kindness.

This book is dedicated to Henry Higgins, a cockney arsonist and psychopath, who was no less than the catalyst to my enlightenment. Ironically, I started out as the teacher and ended up as Eliza Dolittle, the naïve student. Perhaps Henry's unwitting mission was to help others by having me tell our story.

But even before I met Henry, the loss of a sibling in my early twenties had compelled me on a quest to understand what life was all about. Initially, angry at a God who would take my brother away, I rejected religion. Eventually, however, I came to realize that religion, science and philosophy were compatible. The scriptures, after all, form the moral basis of Western civilization. To leave religion out of a quest for the meaning of life, then, would be akin, as Rabbi Lord Jonathan Sacks said, to "not reading the minutes of the last meeting." Similarly, overlooking mysticism and spiritualism would – cribbing the words of John Milton – "bring a famine upon our minds again, when we shall know nothing but what is measured by their bushel."

My passion, which I discovered at 29, was attending ballet classes, which became the conduit for my quest. My first teacher, Ivor Meggido, often incorporated philosophy into his classes. He whetted my appetite for knowledge and inspired my career choice as an exercise therapist, which led me to teaching classes in homes for psychiatric offenders, where I met Henry; nursing homes, where the residents lived out their final furlong, many in a solitary room, dependent and lonely. At day centers, I encountered individuals of all ages with a variety of mental, physical and emotional disabilities. I sought to understand them all through my looking glass of behavioral psychology, Bible studies, philosophy, poetry, Eastern religions, spiritualists, psychics and astrologers.

What I discovered was that my students, whatever their weaknesses or handicaps, were similar at their core. I learned that everyone is valuable, and we are all here for the same reason. But life can be painful, and there are the few who have become so disillusioned that they tire, recoil, stop the ascent, and just collapse in place. Some lose the desire or will to follow the light, choosing to remain in darkness. Others have the ability to heal and change their lives. They are the ones who come to comprehend that life isn't about what happens to us, but about how we handle it. Whatever the limitations of those I encountered, I attempted to explore the universal, simple truths that pointed to the possibility of a meaningful life for them all. What I didn't realize at the outset was that giving to them would illuminate the path to a meaningful life for me. The greatest rewards in life, it turns out, come from giving, the catalyst for receiving. The more I gave, the more came back to me.

If others benefit from this work, Henry's life was not lived in vain. At the very least, he and many other students taught me a fundamental truth: that we do our best only by changing ourselves, not by taking responsibility for others. We change when our minds give in to their craving for communication with our bodies and spirits. This is how we open the power within and make it through life, regardless of our circumstances. Those who don't, leave their suffering untouched. Henry, sadly, was in that group.

Chapter One

Hostel for Psychiatric Ex-Offenders

It is in our darkest moments that we must focus on the light.
— Aristotle

Henry can't see the point any longer. He lies on the road outside the pub. A passer-by tries to pull him to safety. But he doesn't want to get up. He just doesn't care anymore. "What's the point, It's always the same thing," he thinks. "A hand pulls you up and you fall down again, and then again, like a yo-yo. Might as well start fixing again, until the end comes." Like many others, he no longer has any idea what life is about. What is certain is that no life is without challenges, an observation that was a universal truth for Henry and his mates at a hostel for psychiatric ex-offenders. Without exception, they were born into a vicious cycle of pain, violence, and misery.

My introduction to the Hostel was stark. "Is this the hostel for ex-offenders?" I asked a passerby. "That's a terrible place," she replied, immediately casting a shroud on the venue where I was about to lead a physical exercise class. As it was, the "swinging sixties" hadn't made much of an impression on the architect who designed the gray, soulless, stone structure of flat roofs and large windows, which, 35 years later, housed 32 male residents and staff. I could never have imagined what lay ahead within these walls: that I would open my heart, find answers to so many questions, become confident of my worth, develop self-esteem, and find my own true light.

The Kabbalah, popularized by celebrities such as Madonna, explains the concept of light. Its teachings rest on the belief that the world was built on light – the medium of revelation. This light always shines twice. The first light is the hidden light of creation, perfect, infinite, full of potential and inspiration. But then it disappears, leaving darkness and a longing to experience it again. Eventually, we may, but it is never as bright. Could this uninviting hostel be what introduced that light, the one I aspired to seek and follow without knowing where I was going?

It might not have happened. Friends and family tried to dissuade me from taking the job: they believed it was dangerous for a woman to work with disturbed men deprived of female company. Indeed, on its face, the residents were hardly what most would consider an appealing segment of society. According to a study by a psychiatrist from Broadmoor Psychiatric Hospital, "The mentally disturbed offender may be acutely or chronically mentally ill; those with neuroses, behavioral and/or personality disorders; those with learning difficulties; some who, as a function of alcohol and/or substance abuse, have a mental health problem; those where a degree of mental disturbance is recognized; some sex offenders and some abnormally aggressive offenders, who may benefit from psychological treatment – an extremely mixed group." But increased risk of violence, the psychiatrist concluded, was associated only with mental illness caused by psychotic disorder. The actual risk of violence posed by most mentally ill people is in fact small.

A hint of what I might encounter came in a truncated telephone conversation with the person making the arrangements for my exercise class: the chat ended abruptly because an argument in the background was getting out of hand. Although I believed that I knew what I was letting myself in for, I now realize that I was terribly naïve. Here I was, the missionary off to convert the natives to the joys of group exercise. To be sure, I had achieved great success in all my classes to date – including a class comprised of difficult psychiatric patients with whom I had achieved a rapport – and trusted that the formula would work everywhere. In truth, my only previous experience of criminal offenders was in my weekly observations in a Crown Court I attended as a guest of the judge. At the time, capable of putting myself only in the victims' shoes, I believed long sentences were in order for all criminals. Still, I found myself wondering about the backgrounds of the accused.

I recall one tall, good-looking hoodlum, who had terrorized an entire council estate. As he was quite capable of carving up people with a knife, the residents were terrified. In this particular case, a camera caught him robbing a petrol station and threatening the cashier. The judge imposed a 13-year sentence. Several months later, "Buck" was back before the same judge, having twice punched a prison guard who had turned down the volume on his radio, leaving him with a disfigured face and a badly swollen eye. Still, Buck appeared in disbelief when the judge gave him a year for the assault. What struck me, however, was that Buck, and frequently other offenders, looked no different from normal honest folk, including the workers who service our homes. Indeed, most presented as your average Joe, albeit from working-class backgrounds.

Another memorable case was the tough guy who took part in the armed robbery of a building society. He was short, slight of build and small-boned, with dark hair he kept swiping off his face. He made life impossible for his lawyers, shouting out from the dock and repeatedly insulting the authority of the Court. Throughout, his mother, a simple, humble, neatly dressed older "Miss Marple" type, sat quietly by and expressionless, never missing a day. Yet he took no notice of her. The judge sentenced him to nine years, but he left the dock smiling as the guards led him away, failing to acknowledge his mother and oblivious to her ordeal.

At the time, I didn't appreciate the consequences of being confined in a locked prison cell with a stranger. But I can now imagine how torturous it must be to come to terms with the loss of freedom and privacy, the encircling, foreboding walls closing in, the isolation from family and friends, and bereft of so many simple pleasures we take for granted. As Oscar Wilde expressed it in the *Ballad of Reading Gaol*:

Dear Christ! the very prison wall, Suddenly seemed to reel,
And the sky above my head became, Like a casque of scorching
steel;
And, though I was a soul in pain, My pain I could not feel.

As it turned out, the hostel residents usually arrived straight from prison or psychiatric units. They ranged in age from their mid-twenties to pensioners in their seventies. Many had lived there for years and had become institutionalized, so that living on their own was no longer a reality. Many came from dysfunctional homes where the environment had poisoned their self-confidence and self-esteem, their tough veneers frequently masking a deep-rooted inferiority complex. Many suffered with anxiety, often culminating in anger. Few had loving families, memories of loving families, religious or other strong beliefs. In short, they lacked anything resembling a fortifying structure they could fall back on in times of need.

Making things worse, their relationships also seemed doomed from the outset. Themselves emotionally crippled, the women they found attractive tended to mirror their own deficiencies. The upshot was heartbreaking, consisting of repeated disappointment, frustration and anger culminating in disillusion that led inevitably to the desire to escape to yet another magical other. The Hostel, however, allowed them to live without responsibility, sustained entirely by the system. Still, their sense of entitlement knew few bounds: I recall hearing a furious resident ranting and raving because he wasn't getting his "fiver" for the day, as the person in charge had gone home.

The residents were free to come and go as they chose. They occupied a simple bedroom with communal bathrooms. Some residents had their own televisions and stereo music systems, their rooms packed with tapes, CDs and videos. The common rooms that boasted a television and a snooker table were seldom used: the residents seemed to prefer mingling in the relative security of their own rooms, where they were allowed to consume alcohol. The workers who staffed the hostel, in their twenties and thirties, were, at best, not highly qualified. Those in senior positions, who came from the school system where they had taken some counseling courses, were "key workers," responsible for individual residents with whom they met regularly. Some developed a good rapport with their clients, who would look to them for all their needs. Most were pleasant, friendly, and well-intentioned – but at the threshold of their lives, weighed down with inexperience.

Group outings, always in the company of key workers, included visits to museums, parks and other cultural institutions. It was on these occasions particularly that the residents felt that the staff looked down on them, by, for example, eating lunch separately. This separation, and the lost opportunities for staff to bond with their clients, reinforced the feelings of "them and us," and fueled residents' general sense of resentment. Like everyone else, they longed for respect. As they saw it, the distance staff kept on outings only emphasized the societal division.

Residents ate in the large colorless, functional dining hall. They queued for food, as they had done in prison. The regular menu was meat, potatoes and basic English cooking. Vegetables were not in fashion here. Weekends might feature a "fry up" with sausages and bacon for breakfast. Still, it all seemed to suffice, few had experienced variety in their diet, and the notion of "healthy" eating didn't really enter their lexicon.

I led an hour-long exercise class each week. Initially, I proposed to hold it in the dining room, hoping to draw more participation from the residents who came there constantly for hot water or coffee. I wanted to inject life, color and vigor into their black and white world, and hoped my enthusiasm and love of movement would rub off on them. As I saw it, mind, body and spirit were connected. Hopefully, if I could get them to tune into my vibrations, my energy would resonate. But my exercise regimen was not one familiar to the residents. I took them on a journey through their bodies, accompanied by music. I started with deep breathing and relaxing to create an awareness and release of tension. I taught them to isolate their body parts – for example, by moving the shoulder in all directions. We lengthened and shortened each muscle group, strengthened it, and finished off by relaxing.

I was scheduled there for morning sessions. It soon became evident that most of the residents, usually hung over from the drugs and drink the night before, didn't rise until the afternoon. So we moved to four o'clock. On the first day at the new time, six residents drifted in and out. Many stayed on the periphery, coming along merely to see what a new female looked like. I enjoyed their company, and the challenge of getting them to trust me and feel at ease in my presence. I knew it was essential to let go of my preconceived ideas if I was to be at all helpful. I gleaned how critical it was to listen and not just hear and endeavored to "read" their body language. What frequently came to mind was Rabbi Lord Sacks' observations about the significance of the words religious Jews utter before they die: "Hear O' Israel the Lord our God, the Lord is One." When Jews recite these words, they cover their eyes with their right hand. This is not a prayer, but a confirmation that the individual has listened to the word of God: a pre-condition to beseech Him to listen to their prayers. Indeed, my father had often counseled me to turn my tongue 10 times before I spoke. Good advice, as it turned out.

The men I worked with wore their hearts on their sleeves. For my part, I endeavored to become a void that functioned as their sounding board. Opening my heart in this way, I believe, is what led me to respond appropriately to them, despite my lack of experience or instruction in this setting. Indeed, I am among those who believe that human beings are energy fields capable of using their intuition to unconsciously decode others' vibrations. So I never came to class with a fixed routine. I knew what music I wanted to play, and what I wanted to work on. But I allowed the group's mood, manifested in the vibrations I picked up, to dictate the flow of the class.

It wasn't surprising to me that, for the most part, the residents weren't in good enough physical condition to exercise energetically. To be sure, many had frequented the gym in prison, but perhaps merely to spend time outside their cells. So I started the class with a leisurely warm-up, but the men frequently tired quickly and were loath to continue. "Come on, you can do it," I shouted to them. And somehow my charm offensive worked: they stuck with it. We moved on to stretching. Again, I cajoled them. This time it didn't work. In the end, I wasn't able to hold their attention for long and found them nearly impossible to motivate. Although 90 percent were unemployed and had little if anything to engage them, they slowly flitted away, preferring to do nothing.

Eventually, only Henry was left in the dining room with me. He was new here , having recently been evicted from his former hostel. This hostel took him in only because no other suitable facilities were available. I could see from his well-formed shoulders that he worked out a lot and was proud of his appearance. But my class represented a different form of exercise than that to which he was accustomed. Henry was used to lifting weights, boxing and "pumping iron." My exercises were more focused, intended to improve body awareness and control by isolating individual parts. Still, Henry seemed interested. Following my direction, he eased himself into a calmer state. But soon other residents wandered in and out, seeking the refreshments that were readily available in the room. The constant to and fro disturbed Henry, soon evoking a wild, hysterical response. He stood up in fury and stalked off in a huff, only to return in five minutes. But when the disconcerting activity resumed, he promptly lost his temper and left again. His third attempt also culminated in his storming out, apparently out of control, only to reappear yet again 10 minutes later. At that point, an odd-looking man entered. He roamed about, making strange noises, talking to himself, and wiping the walls for no apparent reason. He appeared ready to lash out at anyone who got in his way. But no one took notice, except for Henry, who had just returned to the dining room. At the intrusion, Henry went ballistic, becoming even more anxious, angry and aggressive. His raging mind made his body taut. Clearly, it was time for us to move on.

Chapter Two

One's physical posture is their emotional posture made visible

We ended up in a small, dark ground floor lounge, far removed from the madding crowd. Here I was, then, alone with Henry, about whom I knew nothing except that he seemed somewhat unstable and must have spent time in a prison or psychiatric unit. Yet I could see that he clearly desired and needed help. Eventually, he told me that he wanted to learn to relax. But his concept of relaxation was quite different from mine and had nothing to do with the breathing technique I was demonstrating. Instead, he wanted to talk and me to listen. My only qualification, apart perhaps from an abundance of loving kindness, was a certificate allowing me to work with the elderly, people with disabilities and individuals with special needs. But I had no predispositions or judgments to make, just open ears, and about an hour to spare just then. So I listened to Henry tell me that he wanted a relationship and talk about the female staff he fancied. My response was that he would have to deal with his aggression and tension before he could manage a relationship.

Eventually, I managed to bring the conversation back to movement. As it turned out, Henry didn't walk: he swaggered, and in an exaggerated manner. I asked him to leave the room and re-enter, but with an awareness of the center of his body, walking straight and tall, shoulder blades down and back, head held high, abdomen and spine up, and feet firmly on the ground with each step. He did and liked the feeling of walking with pride. Swagger, I explained, was something we held on to for the support we all needed. But good posture was a much better conduit for control and confidence.

As it was, Henry's body presented as too rigid for exercise.

Better to first relax his mind, so as to loosen up his body. Messages to the muscles, which propel movement, begin with thoughts. Similarly, it's well known that many physical illnesses are psychologically driven. The pilgrims who journey to Tours, France, a place of healing, actually experience chemical changes in their brains that block pain. Similarly, music is a terrific medium for exercise, touching our senses through our hearts and spirits. There is no scientific evidence of energy or life force; however, there is a measurable amount of vibration in the body. Our universe is a mass of frequencies, which carry energy. The higher frequencies are what we hear and see; the lower frequencies are what we perceive through smell, taste and touch. We sense these vibrations through our sensors: ears, nose, eyes, and mouth. Our bodies then convert what our senses experience into an electro-chemical code, neural impulses that drive our bodies and minds. By going into our quiet space, we still the vibrations, allowing the mind to achieve peacefulness and calm. But because not everyone's brain interprets these stimuli in the same manner, differences, often giving rise to disputes, may emerge. The way we perceive things depends on our environment and our experience. If someone in a red shirt has been aggressive to you, the next person who comes along in a red shirt may unconsciously invoke a defensive response.

I spent several weeks studying and practicing yoga in an ashram in Devon run by followers of Guru Amrit Desai. There I learned much from his teachings, which exposed me to Eastern philosophy. And there I learned to find my center, about two inches below the belly button. The Chinese call it the Tan-Tien. Anatomically, it lines up with the midpoint of our five fused vertebrae, making it the strongest part of our body. In spiritual terms, the center represents the place of the internal partner, the Spirit, "where the sun always shines regardless of the external weather of your life." Sitting in the Yoga position, closing my eyes, and concentrating on the center allowed me to feel more in control of my life. It was there that I found my inner sanctuary of peace.

Those who accept the existence of their Spirit, Energy or God are never alone. They are strengthened in the knowledge that they are walking with another whose sole purpose is to guide them to their highest good. It becomes a partnership. There is always someone around with whom to talk. It's a simple technique, but it can work on a cognitive level by fostering awareness of what we're doing and why we're doing it. With sufficient practice, what follows is the possibility of changing old patterns of behavior.

Henry seemed so lonely. I didn't want to say too much, merely to convey the idea that he wasn't alone. I hoped to kindle in him an awareness of a greater power that was always there to guide him – if he surrendered to it and used it as a conduit to overcome his sense of solitude and disconnect. When something is not working out and you find yourself in conflict with your environment or surroundings, I told him, step back, wait, and listen for your inner voice. Do nothing, remain open, and the answers will come. If you're uncertain about what to do, forget about it. Remove the emotion from the situation, don't force a solution, and life will find its way of answering. There is scientific evidence substantiating the existence of this inner voice and its association with the pineal gland, a small pine-shaped endocrine structure found near the middle of the brain where the thalamus halves join, and no blood-brain barrier exists. The structure links to a light-sensing organ known as the pineal or "third eye." René Descartes believed it to be the "principal seat of the soul."

Scientists who have studied creativity and the unconscious workings of the brain have established that we all have the ability to perform astonishing artistic, musical or mathematical feats. Sages have a rare abnormality that helps them to access it. This is why sleeping on a problem may occasionally and unconsciously allow the brain to solve it. For the most part, however, normal brains tend to complicate matters, blocking the unconscious information from seeping through. Encouraging the unconscious processes of the brain, can ameliorate this process.

My session with Henry came to a most satisfactory conclusion. He had been receptive and appeared to have benefited from and enjoyed our time together. We went our separate ways, knowing we would meet again shortly at that evening's Christmas celebrations at the hostel.

Time flew, and evening arrived quickly. The dining room, where the event was taking place, was replete with tinsel, holly and color that blended with the festive feel of the season. The Hostel had provided neatly cut, generously filled sandwiches, and sausages on the central table. A separate bar overflowed with soft drinks. The catering staff had done wonders in turning simple fare into the semblance of a fancy occasion. For good measure, the food was not just ornamental: it actually tasted good. Music abounded, first by way of a small band that entertained on guitar and drums; tapes and karaoke followed. The atmosphere was congenial and warm. Local officials, dressed in suits, and their wives mixed with residents in casual, scruffy attire, mostly worn and pilled jeans or tracksuit bottoms to go with T-shirts and washed-out sweaters. But no one seemed out of place: a good time for all.

Henry arrived much later. Oddly, it was as if we were strangers: no sense of recognition, not even a smile, only a vacant stare and no acknowledgment that we had just spent an hour-and-a-half together. So I circulated, trying to drum up interest in my class. Some of the men were absolutely unapproachable, as though I were contagious. Disconcerting as it was, I just ignored it and moved on. Fortunately, others, who had doubtless partaken of a few drinks before the party started, were in good spirits, amiable, gregarious and welcoming. Their warmth went a long way to offset the brush-offs.

To those who seemed amenable, I introduced myself as the new exercise therapist. Deeper conversation, however, wasn't in the cards. Still, my "charm" got a response out of Richard, who volunteered that he had worked out a lot in prison. He hadn't really enjoyed it, but it helped pass the time. I latched onto him, probing for details of his workouts, but again the conversation didn't go very far. I moved on to Frank, another resident I was meeting for the first time. He appeared to be in his early fifties but could have been younger. As Frank spoke of witnessing his friend's death while serving in the army in Ireland, tears welled up and he began to cry. I was very touched, never before having seen such an outward display of emotion in a mature man, certainly not from the macho type of man Frank represented. Now, he worked as a part-time volunteer in an old people's home. He insisted we had met there, but I knew it to be untrue.

Mike, who had drifted in and out of my class earlier in the day, asked me to dance. We were the only ones on the floor, but no one took notice. Although very drunk, Mike managed to move gently in time to the music. He told me he had never danced with anyone before, which I perceived as flattery given how graceful he was. Still, he seemed to be a genuinely warm person – despite the alcohol, not because of it. But when the band took a break, he disappeared. Fortunately, an older, scruffy looking chap took up the microphone and started singing traditional Irish tunes. All in all, a true spirit of Christmas pervaded: a welcome Christmas, indeed, for those with no Christmas tree.

Chapter Three

Meeting the Residents of Hostel for Psychiatric Ex-Offenders

He who is unable to live in society, or who has no need because he is self-sufficient for himself is either a beast or God.
— Aristotle

It was 1997. The New Year had begun. Henry was my most regular student, never missing a class. But my socializing at the Christmas party had paid off. With up to five residents attending at a time and others coming and going, I moved my exercise class to the common room where I had met alone with Henry before Christmas. Although management clearly noticed my classes' popularity, staff, apparently lacking curiosity or the desire to observe, never showed up. Perhaps what surprised me most was that the classes were popular though they provided no instant gratification, like a drawing at the end of an art class, or something to eat when the sessions ended. After all, an inability to delay gratification marked most of the residents. Emotionally immature and impulsive, they expected results immediately, as if everything resembled instant coffee. These were men of action, not words. So much so that the individual who eventually took over my slot had to lure residents to his anger management workshops with the promise of cigarettes.

Not surprisingly, most residents had difficulty functioning in everyday society. My classes, however, offered them a safe venue for expression. In some ways, the classes came to resemble an Alcoholics Anonymous meeting: the residents talked, I listened, and the exercises intervened, almost incidentally. Over time, I developed a real fondness for these men cast as social misfits, outcasts unable to conform and be self-sufficient. Over time, they dropped their guard and showed me their real selves. What I saw was their vulnerability, which was what made them so endearing. Our conversations, for the most part, were about life on a survival level. As I was there to teach exercise classes, I never instigated these conversations. But my students had a deep need to let it all hang out – so I listened. Although I was the only woman in a room full of mostly hardened men, deprived of female company and pleasure, I never once felt compromised by the gentle, respectful souls that surrounded me over the seven months I worked at the hostel. But when they stepped outside our little island of tranquility, I often heard them screaming at the staff. Were they that different from powerful men who shouted at their subordinates? On a basic level, perhaps they differed little from "sophisticated" people who couldn't control their emotions. Were we all just human beings, in it together?

Yet the residents' existence was a transient one: for the most part, they were going nowhere, without plans or goals. For the unemployed among them, the days were long, seemingly endless. To be sure, they were free, albeit in a self-made prison, vegetating without bonds to the outside world. In *Man's Search for Meaning,* Dr. Viktor Frankl observes that "Life's tasks form man's destiny, and each is unique"; that "No one can relieve man from the way he bears his burden"; and that "A man can either take action, accept his fate, or contemplate." Like chiselers who shape their products, individuals create their lives from the raw materials provided. We are born alone, die alone, and can create meaning in our lives only by ourselves.

I was extremely encouraged by how the men took to me. We had a wonderful rapport and they appeared to trust me as one of them. Although my mandate was to be an exercise instructor and I repeatedly made it clear that I wasn't otherwise qualified, my students were always keen to talk about my philosophy of body, mind and spirit. They clearly preferred it to practicing movement and, almost always, the classes ended in discussion.

Some went so far as to confide that they had been sexually abused as children. Their response strengthened my confidence in my methods – somewhat ironically, as they were in fact exercising very little. I was succeeding, albeit not in the way I intended. But I wasn't a qualified counselor. My stock reply to their revelations was that our past was our past, and we all had to live with today. I explained that living their lives through their disturbed history is what made them sad and angry. I endeavored to bring them back to the moment – to focus on the task in hand, the exercise. In essence, I was repeating what I had learned from books on spirituality and Eastern philosophy: even if we live our lives thinking the past was better, we would be sad, thinking of what we were missing; if we lived only for tomorrow, today was bound to disappoint. Fulfillment and happiness come from living in this present, in this minute, in this moment. In the end, we can only do something about how we feel now, not how we felt in the past. Arguably, by learning to be in the present, we are learning to control the future: when we get there, we will be in that moment. So acknowledge what disturbs you. If you can't do anything about it, accept it. But there are safety valves, and you should use them. Express your anger or other emotion by talking the problem through with yourself. Put your strong feelings in writing, then destroy the paper or delete the file.

I am obsessive about intrusive noise. I can't always mute it, so I've taken to playing calming music to drown out irritating sounds. I try to keep things in perspective, refusing to grant them an importance they don't deserve. I tell myself, "I know I don't like it, but it won't kill me." Is what I'm unhappy about worth tolerating? Sometimes it is and sometimes it isn't. What is certain is that if you can't change something, you must accept it: *ergo,* it becomes worth tolerating because it won't kill you. As it turns out, in the grand design, most things don't matter. The irony is that although it's best to live in the present, we can understand life only by looking back on our reference book of experience. We must ask, "What did we learn from this?" And if we haven't learned anything, the problem will arise in another form.

Speaking for myself, I knew what to do – but I couldn't do it on my own. So I sought help and got it through cognitive therapy, an approach that deals with problems on a conscious, logical level. Left to its own devices, the brain can over-intellectualize. But it needs to be a clear vessel. If we have a problem clearing our mind, we must focus on our intention. If we want guidance, wisdom, or inspiration, we must ask for it. Too much emotional entanglement ruins the connection to inner wisdom. Let the instinct and intuition we all possess be our vehicles to wisdom. To do so, however, we must learn how to connect to our body and feel rooted in it. Using movement and understanding how to control it economically and efficiently is a powerful way to achieve this connection.

Back at the Hostel, my regular followers remained faithful to my classes. George was Welsh and likely in his early thirties. I had no trouble warming to his deep, melodic voice cast in a lovely Welsh lilt. Unfortunately, he was schizophrenic and had recently served a nine-and-a-half-year sentence at a prison where his brother was still doing time. George and Mike, who had asked me to dance at the Christmas party, were inseparable friends. They spent a great deal of their time sitting by the petrol station, tin cups in their hands, looking most pathetic. One day they didn't come to class. They'd been "nicked" by the police for shoplifting but let off with a caution after several hours in the police station.

George hadn't been in the hostel long when he attacked a chair with a knife. He was schizophrenic and complained of voices that wouldn't leave him alone. I had read somewhere that the voices schizophrenics heard were angels' voices, as heard by characters in biblical times. Eventually, I agreed. I came to believe that people surrounded by evil thoughts and deeds eventually succumbed to evil thoughts. I was taught to believe "that there are mischievous forces lurking around us in the universe that can penetrate into the aura of vulnerable souls and cause them to misbehave." Interestingly, amphetamine and other drug users report symptoms similar to those that occur naturally in schizophrenics.

Indeed, many schizophrenics and disturbed people report that they hear voices compelling them to do bad deeds. Dr. Carl Wickland, author of *Thirty Years Among the Dead*, found that there were many "homeless spirits" who did not realize they were dead and who found "the warmth of the human aura as attractive as moths find candle flames." Wickland concluded that "homeless spirits" can possess individuals whose resistance is low, like the insane or those on the verge of nervous breakdowns. Normal, balanced individuals are in little danger of "take-over," just as an occupied house is unlikely to be seized by squatters. Some of these spirits are harmless; others are malicious and evil.

After the knife incident, George was placed under very heavy sedation. He ingested a cocktail of tablets daily and had weekly Valium injections. The combination left him in a zombie-like trance. His chin invariably dropped to his chest as he fought sleep. Sometimes, he just trashed the drugs rather than endure their effect. But throughout, he remained one of my most loyal clients, rarely missing a class. As it turned out, George was intelligent and aware. We discussed his goals, which realistically could be nothing but dreams given his mental state and the drugs. Although he would have preferred to be in Wales with his parents, he remained in London, he claimed, because he wanted help. George was genuinely fond of his key worker, whom he described as caring; and doubtless, George's own warm and loving personality contributed to the relationship. I still remember the affection he conveyed on taking my hand whenever he left class. Still, George did little all day and rarely went out. The only relationships he and the other residents seemed to have were with each other. They all came across, or at least tried to come across, as very macho. They would never admit to a feminine side, and especially to their obvious need for loving kindness from others.

From all appearances, George came from a loving family. His mother lit candles in church weekly for her two errant sons, George's parents visited both him and his younger brother, still imprisoned nearby. George also kept in touch with and sent parcels to his younger sibling. He went home for Christmas when his parents paid for the train ticket. But if it wasn't faulty parenting, what had led George astray? The rough streets of Cardiff's dockland area? His genes? Did his mental condition leave him with real choice? Even in his subdued, medicated state, he was apparently planning another robbery.

As might be expected, violence was a regular part of George's life. He boasted of no less than 100 brawls by which he "made a reputation for myself." The evidence in support was plentiful, mostly missing teeth and a body covered with scars, including one that ran from his ear to his neck. Violence in inner cities, like the docklands of Cardiff, is frequently linked to the need to rise above the surrounding poverty by defending one's status and garnering respect. Challenging authority is one way to do it; so is impulsive and reckless behavior. Indeed, conversations with my group typically included discussions about "the way someone looked at me" or how someone "bumped into me," and how it was necessary to right these "wrongs." Achieving respect through force, however, is a futile endeavor. As Evy Poumpouras wrote in *Becoming Bulletproof: Life Lessons from a Secret Service Agent*, she had learned that she couldn't force others to respect her or see her as their equal. Once she came to accept that, she no longer allowed the opinion of others to govern her self-worth, demeanor, and performance: "The measure of your success should be your resolve to carry out your particular purpose or mission in a way that brings you pride and satisfaction," Poumpouras concludes.

Mike, an alcoholic in his late forties, was sweet-natured, soft-spoken despite his heavy Irish accent. His clothes were bedraggled and torn. He often wore no socks or socks with holes in them, revealing badly sore legs and feet swollen by red blistery pustules and flaky skin. He claimed to have had a wife who worked as a cleaner when he was a security guard, a job he had enjoyed because it included the company of a dog. His children were grown and didn't care to see him. One, he said, was a university student. Every few years or so, Mike went off to Ireland to see his father, who was also a lifelong alcoholic. But Mike claimed he like to read. When his reading glasses broke, I gave him mine, which he returned promptly after securing a new pair. The gesture, and the used paperback book that he gave me to read, touched me.

One day, I left my reading glasses in my car. Mike offered to fetch them: "You trust me, do you?" he asked. Foolishly, I did, and as the minutes ticked away, I realized what the consequences might be. To be sure, Mike was a car thief, but I believed I had built a rapport based on honesty and mutual respect – a rapport I didn't want to undermine by not trusting him with my keys. But if he took the car and injured anyone, I would be at fault. Fortunately, he returned in ten minutes, after what seemed like an eternity. His trustworthiness on this occasion, I believe, had much to do with respect: while some treated him like a leper, I treated him as an equal. Just one week later, Mike didn't show for class. I discovered that a doctor had committed him to a psychiatric hospital for 30 days. I sent a card wishing him well. When he returned after "drying out," he immediately thanked me. It was the only card he had received. Still, the break had been good for Mike. He was calmer, cleaner and less disheveled. And he tried to stay sober, carrying soft drinks with him in place of beer. But it was all for naught; within a week, he succumbed to the alcohol again. Temptation overcame what he had learned in the hospital and his own desire to change. But perhaps that was understandable, as it was in George's case: the Hostel was a den for the very vices they had both hoped to avoid. What it also meant is that my extra efforts with the residents, including frequently staying beyond the hour allotted to my class, were doomed by the circumstances.

Joe looked like an overgrown oaf. His six-foot-five-inch body, featuring arms that were too long and a decided paunch, lacked grace as much as his personality lacked poise. The result was awkward, highlighted by a hunched stance and a head tilted forward to minimize the distance his height created from the person to whom he was talking. Joe was nearing 50 and pined for love and the wife and home he never had – so much so that he asked me to marry him. And he never got over it: when I left the hostel, he refused my farewell hugs and a peck on the cheek. Perhaps he managed to find his comfort elsewhere. Rumor had it that he was one of George's bedtime companions. An orphan from the hard slums of Glasgow, Joe went directly from the orphanage to the army. Dishonorably discharged, he became a road sweeper. An inveterate grumbler, his targets included the Hostel, the government, politicians, the "elite," and society in general. He had been hard done by, he felt, by all of them. An opinionated man, he could be interesting in his conversation, but only until his anger took over – which occurred not infrequently. Staff were often the objects of his invective, and from time to time, he left the hostel to cool off. But after some time on the streets, he always returned.

Joe, like George, was schizophrenic, suffering from delusions and hallucinations. His particular version of the illness produced low motivation and difficulty communicating feelings. Perhaps the frustration of not being able to make himself understood caused his anger. In this way, he resembled most of his co-residents, also unable to express their emotions. Maybe their feelings were so painful that they cut them off merely to function and survive. Indeed, a 1970 study by Dr. Heston found that adopted children born of schizophrenic mothers were more likely to be morally defective, sociopathic, neurotic and to have been discharged from the armed forces on psychiatric grounds. Still, I wondered if destiny, rather than society or genetics, had dealt Joe his fate. Had he, as those who believe in reincarnation assert, chosen the life and environment to which he was born by way of perfecting the weaknesses in his character and repaying his spiritual debt?

I grew particularly fond of another student, Rick. He was 32, five-foot-eight, smallish, and nice looking. He had an engaging manner and winning smile despite the black spaces where some teeth had been. But Rick's history was gruesome: tears filled my eyes when I heard it. His father, not unexpectedly, was alcoholic. His three older brothers raped him when he was nine, then forced him into prostitution. Unsurprisingly, violence imbued Rick's life. He went to prison for robbery and raping a minor, but his sentence was reduced in recognition of the suffering in his formative years. He was, of course, ashamed of his history and alluded to it only in passing. Somehow, however, he had his own television, a stereo, and an impressive collection of thousands of music tapes and CDs, many featuring Elvis Presley. I wondered where he had found the money to buy them and whether they were the proceeds of ill-gotten gains.

Rick attended my classes regularly until his girlfriend, who was also his sister's roommate, moved in with him at the Hostel. Later, the Hostel provided them with a little flat across the street. While Rick benefitted from the loving female companion who seemingly adored him, she was perennially unemployed, and they spent their days drinking. When she was sectioned and sent away, he took to banging his head against the wall at night, like a child. Rick had little self-esteem. He insisted that he was filthy and evil. Nothing I said or did could change his attitude. His arms were badly scarred. One day I noticed a raw wound that he had self-inflicted because, he said, he was so detestable and wicked that he wanted to hurt himself. Would he have been different had his childhood not been snatched away? What was clear was that he would never forgive his brothers. Still, I'll never forget the time he held my hand with so much feeling.

Where and how one grows up influences the way the brain develops, like clay that hardens with time. Inside are wires carrying messages. Without love and security to nourish it, the wiring system goes awry, often irreversibly. Life becomes a constant struggle. In 1977, Dr. Harlow experimented with turning rhesus monkeys into sociopaths by separating them from their mothers. The consequences were lifelong. Harlow discovered that humans and monkeys who do not bond with their mothers become fearful, aggressive, hyperactive and unable to empathize. They see life as black and white.

David, another member of my group, stood out at the hostel. Handsome, well-dressed and clean-cut, he had lived in a respectable middle-class home with his wife and three children – until he burned their house down. It turned out that David suffered from claustrophobia and panic attacks, staying in his room with the curtains drawn until the episodes passed.

Frank, another regular, had a small frame and muscular body that suggested a history of hard physical labor. His face was etched with deep lines and furrows. Like many others in the hostel, he had been sexually abused as a child. Nonetheless, he had a few children of his own scattered around. One day, Frank came to the session with the "good news" that his girlfriend was pregnant. He was overjoyed and crying openly, which was not unusual for his emotive personality. But no one, me included, could share in his excitement. As usual, he had no future plans and never mentioned the woman or the pregnancy again.

Fred was in my group just a few times. He became ill and never returned – one of the older residents, he appeared to be about 60. Emaciated, pale, wobbly and shaky, he was clearly not in good health. An unsettled, itinerant childhood had doubtless contributed to his depression and suicidal ideation. To make matters worse, he was a compulsive gambler who wasted every penny he had at the betting shop.

Pudgy, sweet, polite and gentle, thirtyish Neal looked and behaved like he couldn't and wouldn't hurt a fly. But he had done nasty things to women, something I discovered only after I had spent time alone with him. At one point, I returned from a prolonged holiday to find that attendance was low because two of my regulars had been sectioned and another had moved. So Neal and I had a lot of quality time. On more than one occasion, he mentioned how wrong he believed masturbation to be. I knew that sex offenders often adhere to a strict moral code of behavior, including a rigid approach to sex likely ingrained at an impressionable age. Sex, then, was not to be discussed; it was "dirty" and permissible only in marriage. Things looked like they might improve for Neal when an interview for a part-time job came up. But he never went, explaining that he couldn't "bring himself to it." While I had come to realize that I couldn't rely on what many residents told me, I wondered if he simply hadn't received the support he needed. Perhaps the system couldn't afford what was necessary to make a real difference. Or perhaps it wouldn't have made a difference at all.

Paul, with his bald pate, resembled Yul Brynner. Passionate about yoga, he sported a white T-shirt and navy tracksuit bottoms with a hole in the crotch, leaving little doubt that he wore no underpants. Paul talked and interrupted constantly, chain smoking all the while. I tried to teach him about control. It appealed to him, and eventually he was able to control his endless chatter and smoking, albeit only for a week. Oh, well, I thought, at least he now understood that he could take control if he wanted to. Unfortunately, he moved to another hostel before we could make further progress.

It took me a while to get to know Otis, the only black student in my group, and one of only two black men in the hostel. He was a lady's man, a real charmer, and I never felt comfortable alone with him. When he first came to class, Otis was always high on crack. A real wise guy, it was hard to get a straight answer out of him. When I finally got him on my own, however, I confronted him about his attitude. From that day on – at least in my presence – he evolved from an annoying smart ass to someone with depth. He opened up and began talking about himself. An intelligent fellow who had worked in an office, he had a variety of interests, but could find no one in the hostel to share them with. On the other hand, the class was always more physical when Otis was around. Agile enough to challenge me with feats of flexibility, he loved to play football and go dancing.

One day, Otis showed up with a girlfriend, Sarah, in tow. She seemed very keen on him, which surprised me because the previous week he had professed his love for a woman named Susan. Rarely could I tell if Otis was serious or having me on. For example, he had trouble restraining his laughter when the conversation turned to spiritual matters, but I never discovered whether he found the talk ridiculous or it had touched a nerve. The last time I met Otis, we had a long talk about his meeting my dance teacher, Ivor Meggido. Ivor had danced with the Royal Ballet until an injury stymied his career, forcing him to move on to musicals in the West End. I was hoping that he could direct Otis' innate talent and give him purpose. Our talk was so wonderful that he kissed me on the cheek as we parted. I told the assistant director about it, but she looked startled, told me it was dangerous and that residents were prohibited from touching staff. The following week, Otis was sectioned for six months. I knew not why. What I knew was that Otis had once tried to commit suicide by jumping in front of a train, and I wondered if something similar had happened. However that may be, I never saw or heard from Otis again.

Soon after my last encounter with Otis, a voicemail from my supervisor gave me three weeks' notice, without explanation. But my class numbers were down after a prolonged break during which the hostel had taken many of the residents on holiday to Wales. Unfortunately, the weather had been cold and wet and not a single member of my group enjoyed or appreciated the break. It upset their routine, altered their mindset, and killed the momentum the class had developed.

Chapter Four

Secure and Insecure Attachment

Who is strong is he who conquers personal inclination. He who is slow to anger... (overcoming darkness in ourselves).
— Ethics of the Fathers

To qualify as an exercise therapist for the elderly and people with special needs, I had to study physiology, and also enrolled in a university level class on behavioral psychology. There I learned that the brain craves communication with the body. It achieves this through nerve cells, which in turn affect our organs. When our brains receive a stimulus from our sensory organs, the cells secrete chemicals that drive our hormones. It follows that the first step in making changes to an individual's temperament is to change the way that the individual perceives the events that his or her senses receive. People whose first reaction is to act aggressively, then, need to train themselves or be trained not to feel threatened. One way of doing that is by becoming aware of and avoiding the triggering event.

Endorphins, found throughout our bodies, are natural opiates or narcotics that act as neurotransmitters. Dopamine, an important behavioral chemical, can only be released when the body achieves a critical level of endorphins. Schizophrenics secrete too much dopamine, creating turmoil in their minds. Medicine seeks to treat this condition with drugs that block the dopamine receptors. Endorphins are associated with many behaviors, including crying and laughing. They affect our positive sensations, including listening to music; participating in aerobics; reacting to acupuncture, placebos, massage, near-death experiences, labor and delivery; eating; and playing with pets. But they also have negative associations: with stress, depression, compulsive gambling, trauma, and masochism, and even obesity and eating disorders. Endorphins also affect our immune systems. Emotionally stressed individuals, for example, are more susceptible to colds and influenza; nausea can be an emotional as well as a physiological reaction; and back pain is often connected with insecurity. Ultimately, it seems, our bodies are the barometers of our emotions.

Our feelings serve us most efficiently when we listen to them. But the physical and mental sophistication of mankind means that we frequently lack, or mask, the instincts that animals have to stay in touch with their feelings. Instead, we often rely on anxiety, the main wakeup call to those who aren't in touch with their emotions. Our hearts race, we perspire, and our hands shake. The resultant state of uncertainty allows obsessive thoughts to intrude, turning sadness into anger, fear, disgust and panic – all resulting from endorphin deficiencies. Many unfortunates turn to self-medication, and then addiction, to contain out-of-control feelings, often caused by low GABA, the hormone that inhibits excited brains from going over the top.

Alcohol and other drugs can bridge the gap, both calming and stimulating us. Indeed, the issues experienced by many of the psychiatric ex-offenders at the hostel could be traced to their resort to self-medication. Ultimately, addictions are out-of-control, harmful habits, ways of obtaining rewards without effort. But addictions alter our chemical balance and subvert the normal cycles in our brains' pathways, promoting a compulsion for instant gratification. At the opposite end of the spectrum is happiness, an ideal state of equilibrium that does not allow for negative thoughts. How do we achieve that? Being in control is one of the best ways, as it allows us to cope with stress and enhance our self-belief. And being in control lets us feel good, thereby stimulating a positive neurochemistry. Many of my students lacked this sense of control. I tried to help them acquire better control of their bodies through techniques that directed and isolated their movements. This, I hoped, would encourage them to take greater control of other aspects of their lives.

Psychotherapy is another way to deal with problems of the mind. It seeks a deep understanding of the self. In contrast, the behavioral approach reduces stress levels by changing the way we think. Negative thoughts, such as blame or pessimism, affect motivation and alter brain chemistry. But when people are pessimistic and can't cope, they are more likely to become depressed, either due to their unfulfilled expectations or repression of their anger. It's far healthier to let your feelings out – even if you don't feel like it. Ironically, perhaps, depression is best fought by questioning yourself. The negative thinking that marks depressed individuals is often completely irrational. Therapy teaches them to think more creatively about facilitating change in their lives.

Homeostasis is the system that keeps the body and its chemical balance in equilibrium. That's why the body temperatures of healthy humans and animals is constant, varying only by a few tenths of a degree. Similarly, despite the variations in the diets of populations, blood sugar levels remain fairly constant at around one milligram of sugar per milliliter of blood. The fluid levels surrounding our billions of cells also remain constant, with only modest deviations. On a holistic level, this helps explain how to keep life on an even keel. Consider that the most compatible couples have similar biorhythms, energy drives, and ideally, synchronized body clocks.

Love is defined as a strong attachment bond. The attachment bond we create comes from a physiological need to have social contact and be touched and held. Emotional and physical contact makes all social species feel safe. A secure sense of attachment leads to emotional health by prompting the body to release serotonin and dopamine. Attachment begins with the synchronized systems of mother and child. Babies attune to mothers' voices while still in the womb. An insecure attachment to mother, as might occur in a premature baby, deregulates this synchronistic system. Depriving a child of its mother alters its coping equipment, setting in motion lifelong problems.

Attachment is a basic physiological need. The animal kingdom has critical imprinting periods: birds must see their mother in three to five days; otherwise, whatever else they see becomes "mother" to them. For humans, the first two years of life are critical to attachment. Being normal requires that we be held, touched, feel emotions and experience physical contact from birth on. By contrast, the stress occasioned by early abuse and neglect can overwhelm the serotonin system, jeopardizing our ability to find peace. Put another way, attachment teaches the child to trust. If it's not there, vigilance replaces trust, leaving us unattached or detached. Accompanying all this are feelings of loss of control that can manifest in a host of fears and phobias.

Dr. John Bowlby (1907–1990), a Brit, is the father of the "Theory of Attachment." He believed that accepting that their problems stemmed from early childhood and attachment issues with their mother or primary caregiver allowed people to understand and overcome their problems. Relationship problems, Bowlby found, stem from this failure of early attachment. Indeed, his idea that kindness doesn't spoil children changed the accepted attitude to child rearing. He posited three types of attachment: "secure attachment," which characterizes 50 percent of the UK population, and denotes couples who are accommodating and generous to each other; "anxious attachment," leading to coercive, demanding behavior and anger in 24 percent of the population; and "avoidance attachment," which affects 26 percent and is marked by withdrawal, silence, and a sense that the individual doesn't need anyone else. Some people display a combination of anxious and avoidant attachment. These behaviors, Bowlby believed, stem from early experiences with intimacy or its absence. Understanding that connection, he concluded, would help many relationships.

The fetus, then, is vulnerable to mother's mood. Anxiety, fear, anger, hatred and depression in the mother presage a life of conflict in the developing embryo. A child born into a family of violence, abuse and deprivation, or no family at all, is usually unable to create the neural connections that form the sense of attachment so vital for a mentally healthy life and the development of social skills. Body and spirit suffer as well.

Many offenders and societal outcasts grow up in a violent environment. The violence can be verbal as well as physical, replete with noise, rage, anger, and threats. It becomes the default method of communication. Given their need for instant gratification, many of these poor souls cannot recognize the power of God or prayer. The psychiatric ex-offenders I worked with lacked the motivation, self-esteem and confidence to change. They felt ugly and worthless. But deep in their hearts, many heard and understood their inner voice. They had a great need for love in their deep ocean of darkness and despair where they could do little to grow or change. In prison, inmates from similarly dysfunctional backgrounds, often with undiagnosed personality disorders, surrounded them. On release, they had nowhere to go. They wound up in hostels with others, again, who had similar inadequacies. Their overseers frequently lacked proper training.

Still, a loving adult relationship can overcome early damage. The man who shot President Ronald Reagan underwent a profound personality change after developing a relationship with a woman while in prison. And he's not the only one: there are many examples of prison relationships producing dramatic personality change. They include a man so dangerous that he was kept in solitary confinement for years. When he unexpectedly received a letter from his daughter, life took on meaning, and he set out to improve himself.

The point is that attachments in life provide meaning. When

their relationships are threatened, individuals may sleep badly and become aggressive or clingy. And a stressed relationship affects the immune system: being separated from your loved one makes you ill. As well, critical attachments influence physical maturation as much as they do social, emotional, and intellectual development. Our thoughts, feelings, and beliefs about ourselves and the world affect the "soil" that are our immune systems. The strength of your team of natural killer cells and other disease-fighting cells within your immune system are linked not only to what you eat, how you exercise, and other lifestyle choices but also to how you manage stress, relationships, old traumas, what you believe and how you see and understand yourself.

Back to Henry, then, whose troubles could perhaps have been traced to a deregulated stress system resulting from the lack of an early attachment bond caused by his mother's absence due to a severe post-natal depression, and his father's alcoholism. He also had little contact with his brother, himself an alcoholic. The upshot was that Henry couldn't trust anyone, rendering him unable to surrender to his feelings and let go regardless of the degree of attention and commitment devoted to him. His world view was black and white: all he saw were predators intent on bringing him down. Like Henry, many of my students didn't recognize warmth because they hadn't received it in childhood. But Henry was different: he said he wanted to change. My support and encouragement helped instill a sense of calmness and well-being, a healthy substitute for the drugs that were his usual fallback – but only for a while. More particularly, Henry's lack of attachment in childhood had altered his blueprint. He was hardwired, and the damage, as it turned out, was permanent.

Chapter Five

Studies of the Biology of Behavior

James Springer and James Lewis, born in 1939, believed that their identical twin had died at birth. When they were reunited, they discovered that they both had the name James. Each had married and divorced a wife named Linda, married a woman named Betty, and had a dog named Tony. Both enjoyed carpentry and mechanical drawing and had spent family holidays on the same beach in Florida. They were each six feet tall and weighed 180 pounds. They held their table knives the same way, and they had similar gestures, voices and bodies. Both men had elaborate workshops where they made miniature picnic tables and rocking chairs, followed stock car racing, and hated baseball. Their wives said they were both romantics who left love notes around the house, but also anxious sleepers who ground their teeth at night and bit their nails to the quick. Both had high blood pressure, and both believed, without medical confirmation, that they had experienced heart attacks. Both had had vasectomies, hemorrhoids, and a lazy eye on the same side. Their personalities were remarkably similar. Their story, and the many twin studies that produced similar results, cannot help but make us ponder how much free will we really have.

From conception, children are stamped with their behavioral makeup and 50 percent of their personality. Baby boys are more fragile and vulnerable than girls and need more attention in the first years of their lives because their brains are less mature by six weeks at birth. Boys are more likely to suffer neurological disorders when their biological weaknesses are made worse by insensitive treatment. In patriarchal societies such as Arabia, boys grow up physically and emotionally stronger. Everyone has some genetic predisposition to mental and physical illnesses, including autism, schizophrenia, phobias, neuroses, vulnerable immune systems, cancer, and respiratory and environmental diseases. Stress can cause these weaknesses to become acute. We all possess free will but struggle to choose who we become. A traumatic childhood causes repetitive patterns, but these can be arrested and changed. Parents affect their children's motivation and self-esteem. Once their nurturing exceeds a minimum level, they have little measurable impact on their children's intelligence, interests and personality.

Ideal mental health means being able to function adequately; responding appropriately to the situations life presents; satisfying social and occupational roles; resisting stress; actualizing potential fully; making healthy individual choices; and perceiving reality accurately. Mental illness has physical, environmental or organic bases such as brain damage, genetic defects or problems in neurotransmission. If genes are faulty or the brain is damaged, an imbalance occurs in the concentration of neurochemicals, leading to disordered behavior. Mental disorders are treated with drugs, or in extreme cases, with psychosurgery and electro-convulsive therapy. Mental illness can be psychotic or neurotic. Psychosis affects the entire personality; neurosis affects only part. Symptoms such as rage, impulsiveness, violence and irritability that populate these disorders all relate to an imbalance of chemicals. When a person reacts emotionally, high chemical levels produce thrill seeking; low levels engender depression and detachment. Some chemicals interact with each other to control fear and anger, but do so differently in psychopaths, whose normal ratios tend to differ from the norm. Ratios in men and women also differ. Otherwise, societal factors can affect chemical balance. Those who perceive themselves as victims and are sensitive to slights or unintentional unfairness may have high levels of certain chemicals that cause them to imagine hostility when it doesn't exist. This was certainly the case at the hostel.

I guessed that Henry suffered from psychopathic personality disorder – a conclusion that was affirmed long after I arrived at it. As a rule, psychopaths present a repetitive pattern of cruel, sadistic and brutally violent behavior. They are pitiless, ruthless and without remorse. Henry, for example, told me he had a dog that he tortured. At law, psychopaths are responsible for their acts, but they cannot be treated successfully. The fact that they may be under the care of psychiatrists merely leads them to consider themselves ill and not responsible for their actions.

I met many students with autism, a form of mind-blindness that manifests across a wide spectrum. Ultimately, autism is an inability to intuit from verbal or social cues. An autistic toddler, for example, may not respond to common facial expressions. Language is literal to autistics, so they are unable to tell lies, understand jokes, or make sense of cartoons or figures of speech. For the most part, they anchor in the physical world, preferring to play with real objects as opposed to daydreaming or playing make-believe. Most fascinating among autistics are individuals who exhibit mild forms of the condition, such as Asperger's syndrome. Often highly intelligent, they can be socially inappropriate. They are the kind of people who focus on details, have exceptional memories and are predictable and logical. They will memorize the Latin names of objects, are fascinated by timetables and skilled with computers, but can't gossip or enjoy popular soap operas. They want friends but have no concept of what it takes to establish and maintain a relationship. Further on, we will meet Gerry, who was obsessed with politicians and politics, and visited the House of Commons regularly to watch debates. But he couldn't relate to his co-residents where he was housed, except for one individual who was very disorientated. In that relationship, Gerry was overprotective and looked after him as one would a child.

Many of the psychiatric ex-offenders whom I encountered had been sexually abused and deprived as children. Over time,

I came to see how many of their crimes were a repetition of their own experiences. Robert Maudsley, one of Britain's most notorious killers, was an extreme example of childhood deprivation. He was brutally beaten by his father and locked in a cupboard for prolonged periods. He has been deemed so dangerous that he has been in solitary confinement for over 20 years. On the whole, psychopaths like Robert have had extraordinarily difficult family backgrounds: rarely do they emerge from secure and stable family settings. Children who have been sexually abused often lose the ability to trust. While the illicit bodily contact can induce temporary affection and pleasure, shame, guilt, fear, helplessness, and anger almost always follow, undermining victims' ability to feel in control of their lives and seeding the fields of depression. The lack of trust also hinders victims' capacity to develop positive personal resources, ambition, and confident life plans. The helplessness that pervades them retards the emotional progress they need to master their life. Instead, they rely on avoidance, denial, and other maladaptive defenses that do not serve them well in coping with life's stresses. It's as if they were bound hand and foot, and blind. But, according to *Medical News Today,* the helplessness is learned: "Learned Helplessness is a state that occurs after a person has experienced a stressful situation repeatedly. They come to believe they are unable to control or change the situation, so they do not try – even when opportunities for change become available."

Men and women cope with stress differently. Men with rigid childhoods can lack satisfactory emotional responses, and instead may rely on the show of power that characterizes sexual abusers. Others become victims: unable to assert themselves because of their low self-esteem, they attract the very people who are prone to exploit them. In a survey of 200 prostitutes, 60 percent suffered childhood abuse at the hands of a father figure. Some 90 percent presented with multiple personality syndrome.

As well, 60 to 80 percent of schizophrenics had suffered early sexual abuse. But depression can also be genetic, caused by less active neural connections that impede the benefits of natural mood hormones. Still, although major depression, particularly in women, can run in families, it often seems to be a response to personal conflicts, emotional traumas or past family problems.

Many other environmental influences are also at work fomenting mental illness. The universe resonates at mass frequencies that carry energy. Our blood vessels are sensitive to these electromagnetic waves. At the beach, on a mountaintop, or in the face of an oncoming storm, the wind can carry negative ions – electrically-charged molecules floating in the atmosphere. When their concentration is low, they can drive down serotonin levels, so that headaches, nausea and dizziness proliferate. In abundance, these ions improve mood, cognitive abilities, and well-being, among other things.

Ants and crabs have sensors that detect negative ions. Black beetles pick up ripples that prevent them from bumping into each other. Living things tune into frequencies that were advantageous to their ancestors. For example, bees see light and the color of flowers at higher frequencies than we do; snakes see their prey at lower frequencies; dogs hear 44 times better than humans and have a much keener sense of smell; and rodents also have very acute smell receptors. Humans perceive sight in the higher frequencies and touch in the lower range. Environmental energy transfers a biological electro-chemical code through our sensors to the brain. But the eye, for example, filters the information because it sees much more than the brain can absorb. Optical illusions can be the result. Our reality, therefore, is based on what stimulates our sensors and how our brain interprets the messages it gets. But our beliefs and desires can also affect our interpretations. This being said, it's critical that our sensors receive appropriate stimulation in the early stages of our development; otherwise, they shut down. Environmental problems such as poor nutrition, allergies and toxins can also affect sensory perception. The endogenous rhythms created by the earth's rotation and lunar tidal cycles, which affect the environment, play a part as well. All these rhythms impact how we adapt. Birds migrate, animals hibernate, and plants grow and shrink seasonally. As we evolved, our biorhythms linked to light bio fields such as earthquakes and sunspots, affecting our sweat, tears, semen, and sleep. In the latter case, Circadian rhythms do not synchronize with our biorhythms, meaning that our hormones are not in temporal balance.

Memory is the process by which we store information. How well our nerve connections function determines how well we do it. Each time a sequence of nerve junctions experiences a particular type of sensory signal, it becomes more capable of transmitting the same signal going forward. Over time, even signals generated within the brain itself can cause the transmission of impulses: in such cases, we may think we're experiencing a sensation, but we're really only experiencing the memory of it. As time moves on, the conscious thought processes of the brain compare new sensory experiences with stored memories. This process helps us select what is important in the new information and helps determine where our brain channels the information for future use, including bodily functions. Short-term and long-term memory also differ: short-term memory takes in what it makes sense of, and long-term memory stores events by meaning. The upshot is that we sculpt and carve the connections between neurons, literally creating our brain's design through our mental processes and responsive habits.

An individual is in control only when the brain is engaged. The brain is at its most powerful when it is focused, without distraction. This is when we form the strongest pathways and connections, the ones easiest to access over time. Our unconscious, by contrast, directs behaviors over which we have no control, like reflexes. Therapy and drugs, however, can control conditioned behavior and effect significant behavioral change. So can the triumph of the will, the focused mind's capacity to overcome disabilities and handicaps by accessing the brain. Motivation is critical here. While sensory pathways to the brain can't be regenerated, the brain's complexity is such that it can sometimes find a way around them.

So, it is possible to change. But it is a gradual process that cannot be forced. Life must be lived by experience: the greater our awareness of what is actually going on, the greater the ability to take control of our lives. Controlling our lives and accepting what we cannot change are the keys to healthier and happier living. Early diagnosis of tell-tale symptoms of violence, followed by therapy during childhood, can divert young and wayward brains from paths that lead into the heart of darkness. In essence, "caring, rather than ... persecution, makes sound biological sense. Biology offers a remedy (to violence)."

Shirley was 18 months old when her parents' marriage broke down. Her mother took her abroad for a trial separation. When she returned home six weeks later, Shirley's father moved out and her parents "shared" her. Shirley spent Friday nights to Sunday evenings with her father and his parents in their comfortable home. But when Shirley "wanted her Mummy," her grandmother sent her into another room to cry alone until she became "happy." She wasn't allowed to call her mother. Eventually, Shirley developed a phobia called separation anxiety disorder, a phobia that extended to any time away from her mother's home, including holidays and air travel. She had years of therapy, which helped some. But when her mother remarried many years later and moved out of the home they shared, Shirley felt abandoned again: her traumas worsened, and severe depression set in. When her condition didn't abate for two years, it became acute. Shirley saw a psychic, who explained that Shirley's trip abroad as a baby during her parents' trial separation had caused her fear of flying. Her brain, which was aware of the domestic problems, reinterpreted the experience and turned it into "fear of flying." Although her fear had nothing to do with planes, it was how Shirley memorized the experience. Shirley also tried weekly sessions of cranial osteopathy, a gentle, subtle treatment aimed at releasing stress and tension. The therapist helped her realize that, whereas she had always blamed her mother for the eight traumatic years in which her father and grandparents had blocked her access on weekends, it was she who was reenacting her feelings in the present. The realization went a long way to improving Shirley's state of mind – but the scars remained.

Still, the progress she made exemplifies the triumph of the will – the focused mind's ability to overcome disabilities and handicaps by continued resort to the brain. Shirley had to see her memories and emotions for what they were, her current sense of reality. The only way to change them was to understand that her fear of airplanes was the memory of that journey away from home and family. Shirley had become insecure and lacked confidence because her neural system had been so stressed during her early development. Now that she saw the picture for what it was in the moment, she coped and felt better. But, as is the case for many victims, she remains prone to learned helplessness instead of developing confidence. Shirley, now a mother herself, risks overprotecting her children as she tries to shelter them from the feelings of abandonment that she imagines they will have when they leave home. So ingrained are her memories that they can still make her feel ill.

We can't effect change without accessing the subconscious where our troublesome feelings originate. Our behaviors, attitudes, thoughts, judgments, and prejudices all emerge from seeds planted in the subconscious. From birth on, we expose children's minds to opinions and prejudices which become the seeds of the traits they present as adults. The subconscious, after all, cannot resort to the power of reason. It is not a part of the mind that we use to make decisions in life. But there are therapies that address the subconscious. At their core is learning to love oneself. When positivity sprouts in the subconscious mind, it will become ingrained in time. The feelings we have about ourselves can change and manifest in a more secure, assertive, and loving being. And the more we love and respect ourselves, the more we transmit these feelings to others.

Hormesis describes the body's strengthening response to low doses of stress. A piece of steak needs a bit of seasoning, but add too much and, it becomes inedible. Similarly, a bit of stress is good, too much is not. Endurance is the ability to bear whatever life throws at us and to keep going no matter how hard it gets. Delving into an individual's early years can often tell us how much endurance that individual will have.

Chapter Six

Dysfunctional Homes and their Outcomes

Emotion, which is suffering, ceases to be suffering as soon as we form a clear and precise picture of it.
—Spinoza

As a ploy to get my attention, Henry always arrived as the others were leaving for the evening meal. He encouraged me to help him. He told me he wanted to change and felt I was the only one who could help him do so. What I had seen of most of the relationships staff generally had with residents convinced me that he had a point. He responded well, and I noticed a big change in him very quickly. He became more open, communicative, and friendly. He was interested in everything I had to say and even tried to do the exercises. He became conscious of his posture and tried to avoid swaggering, instead standing straight and tall. On the whole, he seemed bright, keen to learn, and anxious to improve himself. Nothing about him suggested he was slow or had learning difficulties.

What I did notice on a few occasions, however, was that Henry's eyes rolled around in his head. It wasn't long before I realized that he was addicted to cocaine. Although I had no exposure to "users," those glassy eyes were hard to miss. And I learned a whole new vocabulary: Henry's "draw" was the form of his purchase, a small amount of cocaine rolled up in a cigarette that cost about ten pounds; "gear" referred to the drugs; and "geezer" was simply a bloke.

Overall, Henry appeared to be a textbook case of an individual from a dysfunctional family living in poverty in the East End of London. As his father was an alcoholic who never worked and couldn't pay the bills, the family ended up homeless. Meanwhile, his father battered his mother and punished his two young sons harshly. He often sent the boys to bed without tea, which, sadly, was their entire evening meal. Henry did have a close relationship with his mother. She was apparently supportive, and he visited her regularly. But after giving birth, she suffered from severe post-natal depression that culminated in a nervous breakdown in Henry's early years. The breakdown left her emotionally unavailable to him during that critical bonding period when babies learn to socialize and trust. This parental anger and indifference when he was most vulnerable probably scarred Henry for life, rendering him an ever-angry narcissist and bully, prone to grandiosity. The absence of satisfactory bonding with his mother could also have led to sexual problems and an inability to form satisfactory relationships later in life. To cope, Henry likely developed primitive defenses of hostility and seeming indifference to others – a sort of learnt helplessness.

The undue stress to Henry's neural systems as his brain was developing probably lowered his serotonin levels. He lacked the balanced serotonin that is crucial to a sense of well-being, good self-esteem and self-control. Not surprisingly, Henry was the classroom bully at school.

Emotionally unequipped to deal with his problems, Henry reacted with anger at the slightest provocation. He never learned to negotiate, compromise, delay gratification or control himself. His teachers didn't have time to cope with his disruptiveness, and, as is so often the case, branded him as of low intelligence. This classical pattern of delinquency also marked Henry's teenage years. He played truant frequently, began shoplifting and committing other petty crimes, and got into smoking, drinking and drugs. By the time he was legally permitted to leave school, he still could not read or write. Although he had been working with his uncle on cars for several years, he could recognize the different models only from their badges. Still, life was good, with cars, money, girls and clothes readily at hand.

At 21, Henry took up with a 19-year-old girl. They parented a daughter. A few years later, everything was gone: the money, the girl, the child, the cat and the happiness he remembered. Henry was now a heroin addict, in and out of prison for drug related offences. The opiates in heroin replenished his brain's natural shortage, and so the drug helped him control the rage and anger stemming from his childhood trauma.

Violence was always a big part of Henry's life, so much so that all his teeth were gone, albeit replaced by a false set. His fights also produced a broken arm and a broken leg, an antagonist had bitten off the top of his ear, and teeth marks scarred his face. Another opponent hit Henry in the head with a paving stone, knocking him cold. He spent three months in a coma, eventually awakening in hospital. The injury caused massive brain hemorrhaging, complicated by his use of heroin. Doctors estimated his chances of recovery at no more than 50 percent. When Henry emerged from the coma, he was childlike and had to relearn simple tasks such as washing and dressing. His speech was so slurred that he required two years of therapy. And he would suffer from severe headaches that made gainful employment difficult for the rest of his life.

Henry's anger erupted at the hostel when he lost his temper and hit another resident. The only reason he wasn't expelled was that the authorities could find no place for him to go. The second incident occurred when an intruder entered the hostel at night and tried to break down Henry's door and attack him. Apparently, someone Henry had crossed had sent the assailant to kill him. The police came, but the culprit got away. For a while, Henry was in mortal fear for his life, but breathed easier when he learned that the perpetrator had himself been knifed to death.

About this time, I started having premonitions about Henry. I was attending spiritual enlightenment classes at a College in south London. The class leader channeled a spirit who I "asked" about these premonitions. Henry and I were linked, he explained, as if an invisible string connected us. This type of connection, he added, defied explanation and could be temporary. No surprise, then, that I really looked forward going to the Hostel every week. Although the place featured, among others, a pedophile, a rapist, robbers, arsonists, burglars and assorted violent criminals, I couldn't see or feel the evil surrounding me. Instead, I saw ignorant, love-deprived victims: simple men of simple needs unable to help themselves or allow others to help them. Most had given up: hope had long been forgotten. To be sure, some might have thought me naïve, but I was operating out of loving kindness and the residents returned it to me in abundance. As I see it, evil is the conscious or unconscious intention to do harm, something that resides in us in the form of ignorance and false thinking. Evil's attraction, for those who have not learned the strength and force of the soul and natural law, is the power it gives us to impose our will on others. Evil is the sole source of power for inadequate people, and most of them commit evil as a result of deep frustration, pain or suffering. Those so afflicted blame their circumstances on others, building up tension that frequently leads to anger and hate that distorts reality. Psychopaths and others who have lost control, for example, may identify as predators.

We are all born with free will and the capacity to do good and evil. The evil man cannot necessarily be distinguished from anyone else on the street. Evil is not genetic: the spirit does not position itself to effect evil, and the brain is not so programmed either. But a negative environment during crucial stages of development, especially around the age of two, can block neural connections and make life a struggle. Research suggests that the biological flaws that put children most at risk for future violent behavior creep into the brain during developmental windows in which the brain and the nervous system are extremely sensitive to environmental and emotional insults that shape an organism's response to stress. Mother's absence is perhaps the most damaging form of abuse and neglect. A young child or infant lives in constant sensory agitation. To channel that arousal into calm and well-being, the child ordinarily relies on love and physical contact with mother, father, grandparent or caregiver. Absent this attention, the young withdraw, frequently ignoring the outside world and stimulating themselves by repetitive rocking, self-clasping and other stereotypic movements. Children who suffer abuse or torment at this sensitive stage are unable to cope with life's stresses as adults, because the difficulty they have controlling their feelings makes anger their most frequent reaction. Many of these individuals never learn empathy. Unable to read the emotions of others, they stumble into conflicts that emotionally literate children would avoid. By the time they enter school, it may already be too late for them to find the tools they need to build healthy relationships. For those whose hearts are so fractured that love cannot flow, drug abuse often provides the necessary glue by temporarily freeing them of the reality and pain that are their lives. Unfortunately, the nervous systems of younger people seeking this form of escape frequently feature chemical trip wires leading to extreme, unpredictable violence. Their only salvation, as I will elaborate upon later, is spirit, for no measure of abuse or neglect can ever destroy the power that spirit has and gives: even in a severely damaged being, the soul only leaves the body at death.

Chapter Seven

The Psychopath

The important thing in life is not the victory but the contest; the essential thing is not the victory but the contest; the essential thing is not to have won but to have fought well.
—Baron Pierre de Coubertin, 1908

I had just finished my class and was about to drive off when I saw Henry returning to the hostel. We spoke, and he eventually settled down in my car. We bought a newspaper to see how his reading was progressing. From the time I found out about his inability to read, I had spent the end of each session, when we were alone, practicing reading with him. I made tapes of songs he liked and wrote out the words for him to follow. Henry asked me to give him a lift and wait in the car while he completed an errand. I only realized afterwards that I had been stationed at the home of a drug dealer on a council estate. This was a huge disappointment to me. Henry had really opened up, acknowledging that I had made a great impact on his life. When I left him, however, I couldn't stop crying. I had just been demoted from the spiritual enlightenment class I had attended with regularity and couldn't understand why. Henry's manipulation gave me the answer: until that moment I hadn't truly believed in the efficacy of my work and the power of spirit.

I returned to the Hostel the following week with new-born confidence, only to discover that I had been given notice: there were only three sessions left. Despite the letdown, I concluded I had come to the end of my purpose there, for myself as well as the residents. But Henry became distressed and morose when he heard the news. Without my support, he feared his remission from adversity would end – and that he would resume breaking tables and chairs to alleviate his rage and frustration, as he had done so often in the past. I knew then that I couldn't desert him. Going forward, I suggested we meet in Covent Garden, on Sundays. Although Henry was born within the "sound of the Bow Bells" and raised in East London, he had never been to Covent Garden. Like many other people of his "station," he felt intimidated by the surroundings, people and prices that populated the "West." But he clearly felt like the "Connecticut Yankee in King Arthur's Court" as we walked along the Mall and through St. James's Park, around to the Palace of Westminster, Westminster Abbey, up Whitehall, and past Downing Street. I even showed him around the lobby of the Savoy hotel. "What sauce to go into the Savoy of all places?" he muttered as we left. I was thrilled to bring him so much delight, and that a new world was opening to him. I understood the harshness of his previous life, how he had retained the violent memories of rejection and fear. I endeavored to replace them with positive experiences. Many months later, Henry remarked that, by treating him as an equal, I had shown him the light when he felt he had hit bottom again. I tried to help Henry understand that sitting in a Rolls Royce wasn't the measure of self-esteem; far more important were a sense of honor and recognition that only he had the right to value himself.

One day, I suggested we go to Kenwood for an outdoor concert on the lawn. It was a cool August evening, albeit not unpleasant, and a bit of rain greeted us as we arrived. After a while, Henry's teeth started chattering and he began trembling. But it wasn't the rain or the cold: he told me that he had been taking methadone in an attempt to kick his heroin habit. I took him home. On our next encounter, the fourth after I left the hostel, I gave Henry an ultimatum to give up drugs. Unless he did, I explained, there was no other reason to continue our relationship: I couldn't help him unless he made a real effort. The date was August 9, 1997 the 26th anniversary of my brother's passing, and I emphasized the moment's importance for us both. This would be the day, I told him, when he took control of his dependency and was reborn. Without realizing it, I had made Henry – who was the same age as my sibling was when he died – the brother I had lost, a substitute for a relationship I sorely missed. It was nothing less than a classic case of subconscious transference, a redirection of feelings or desires for one person onto another.

We both knew how difficult it would be for Henry to give up drugs, which were part of his environment at the hostel. Fortunately, he was attending a drug rehabilitation center daily, and he also understood how different he would be and feel if he succeeded. In the end, I was amazed at how easily Henry, with the assistance of methadone, let go of his addiction. He developed enthusiasm and confidence. His relationship with his own key worker improved dramatically, and he even attempted to help other residents by becoming a key worker himself. Still, Henry was a loner who had no friends among the 30 residents. I encouraged him to befriend George. He did, and Henry took George to Covent Garden and St. James's Park. To be sure, George was hardly a perfect companion given his tendency to stop for a pint at every pub along the way. But things seemed to be working out.

Knowing how important it was to stay in touch, I bombarded Henry with letters weekly. Though reading was difficult for him, my expectations of him and his abilities were growing all the time. When we met, I always kissed his cheek, put my arms around him, and touched him often – all in friendship, which he understood. I was trying to break down the walls he had built around himself. He had mentioned that he fancied me while at the Hostel, but never showed his feelings in any other way. To his credit, he always behaved appropriately.

The end of August marked Henry's birthday. I invited him to a showing of *Pygmalion*. He knew the *My Fair Lady* story and gladly came along. This was the first time he had been to a theater and certainly had never experienced such plush velvet seats. He seemed to enjoy the play, but as was his wont, never betrayed his feelings about the experience. Even when I took him to a casual restaurant afterward, he never appeared overwhelmed, as I am sure he was. If the truth be told, I was probably enjoying myself even more than he was, basking in the emotional reward of giving a new breath of life to another human being.

I took two weeks' vacation. But the Henry I returned to wasn't the same person I had left. He wasn't in a hurry to see me. When he did, three weeks later, he was agitated and out of control. We had met as usual after my dance class and spent a long time at the park. He was disappointed when I suggested we get some hamburgers. "Hamburgers aren't food," he said, so instead I took him to a cheap, but pleasant buffet style "eat all you want" Chinese restaurant. We sat outside on the warm September evening. But after about 30 minutes, Henry burst out with "Where's the food?" at the waiter – loudly and rudely enough to make those around us turn their heads. I didn't like what I was seeing, but I had invested so much in him, I wanted a return on my time and energy. I wanted to win. But Henry had taken to perceiving me in a different light. When I dropped him off at the tube, he was, for a fleeting moment, the person I had grown to love. But, ultimately, that moment brought to mind the vision of a dark boarded-up house: occasionally, a shutter might swing open, allowing a glimmer of light to emerge, only to quickly close again. The relationship became even stranger. It remained devoid of gratitude or reciprocity even as Henry's expectations about my availability – and anger when I didn't meet those expectations – persisted. Finally, an unpleasant telephone conversation ended with his hanging up on me.

A year earlier, Henry lost part of his ear when someone bit it off in the course of a scuffle. He was seeking damages from the Criminal Injuries Compensation Board. Sometime after our aborted telephone conversation, he contacted me, asking me to provide a character reference. I explained that a character reference was irrelevant: the determination of his award depended on the damage or loss he had suffered in the attack. Instead, I wrote a letter emphasizing the effect that the loss of hearing had on an individual who was as fastidious about his appearance as Henry was. On his insistence, and against my judgment, I also sent a character reference. That was the last I heard from him for a while, but eventually, Henry responded to a Christmas card with an endearing phone call. Yet again, though, I didn't hear from him again for two months. One evening in February, when London was at its grimmest and grayest, loving thoughts overtook me. I decided not to contact him – but the telephone rang, and there he was. Henry told me that he had left both the hostel and the drug rehabilitation center. He was living in his uncle's council house in East London. Divorced and 49 years old, the uncle was a minicab driver who headed for the pub right after work and always returned home drunk. Henry was uncomfortable there: alone day and night, he didn't rise until midday for fear of disturbing his uncle, who was perpetually sleeping off hangovers. My first reaction to Henry's call was, "Why do I even need this in my life?" But I couldn't help thinking about the spiritual connection between my thoughts of Henry and his culminating call. Spiritualists believe that any situation that presents itself is there for a purpose. The spirit contacts the body by way of our emotions, offering what we need for growth. Accept the challenge or forego the opportunity until and if it does come around again.

Soon after, Henry phoned again and asked if he could see me. When he arrived at my flat, he appeared disturbed and depressed. Alone with nothing to do all day, he now missed the companionship in the Hostel, whose residents he had complained about so regularly. But he wasn't welcome back at either the hostel or the rehabilitation center. A few days later,

Henry turned up at my flat without notice. I wasn't pleased and read him the Riot Act: he was not to come to my home without an invitation. Through it all, Henry grew increasingly aggressive, making it more and more difficult for me to help him. He refused to take responsibility for his situation, even blaming the Hostel for his departure. The only person he cared about, he said, was himself. Finally, he stormed out of my flat in a temper so intense that I was concerned he might damage the building on his way out. I knew then that I had made a serious error of judgment in allowing him to my flat in the first place, putting myself and my neighbors at risk. I also knew that I had not been aware of or let myself believe who Henry really was.

Still, I wondered whether my friend Jade, a psychic and counselor, could help Henry. I arranged for her to see him, warning her of his background. Perhaps she could give him hope. But I couldn't fight off my feeling that he was beyond my abilities to assist, perhaps because he now reminded me of a recent incident involving Ivan, another favorite student. I had worked with Ivan in a mental health group, which he ceased attending quite suddenly – surprising because of the enthusiasm he had persistently demonstrated. Sometime afterward, I bumped into Ivan on the street. But this wasn't the Ivan I had known: he was clearly severely disturbed and displayed profound symptoms like rapid speech, constant repetition and a failure to relate, that all pointed to autism. Although we were in a public place, I was frightened, worried that he might strike me. Obviously, the unexpected encounter and conversation about his absence from class had triggered repressed or stressed aspects of Ivan's personality. Like Henry, he had morphed abruptly from a model student to what now seemed to be an unsalvageable case.

Henry was as surprised to see me as I was to see him when we both showed up the next day at the pre-arranged locations where we would embark on our 10-minute walk to Jade's place.

Uncharacteristically – at least for someone who took immense pride in his appearance – he looked as if he had spent the night on the street. He was ravenous, and thankful for the tea and cheese sandwiches Jade offered. After a bit of chat, I left. With Henry's consent, I left behind a recorder to tape the session.

Jade focused onto Henry and "tuned" into his vibration. She instantly picked up and identified someone full of ideas and struggling to move forward, hampered by noises and static in his head. She could "feel" a sensation of screaming, screeching sounds blocking his progress, until he finally tires and falls down. The picture she painted was of someone racked with inner turmoil, preventing him from finding who he really is. She endeavored to find a solution and advised him on ways to practice calm to slow his thoughts and actions down and think before he acts.

She could see the violence and cocoon of darkness that surrounded him, like an East End drama. His memories were locking him into his past, perpetuating tension and fear. He was constantly on guard, waiting and watching for the next knife, so ingrained were all the beatings he took and the violence that was his life. She saw the move to his uncle's home. She encouraged him to go for walks in nature in the park, to go fishing, as he had done in his past. She could "hear" the loud noise in his head repeating the sense of failure, futility and violence, his subconscious underlying feeling of the pointlessness of his life.

"That's how I feel, what's the point" then he descends into depression. She asked what it is that makes him feel it's pointless? She asks, "there's always that thing with you, what's the point? What is it that does it to you?"

He told her of his life spraying paint on cars in a body shop. She encouraged him to become a mechanic as he loved cars and enjoyed working with his hands but was aware he needed to work for himself and couldn't be employed or take orders. "I can't spray anymore, it affects me head, I used to love that smell." She advised him to find goals, ambition and something he loves to pull him forward. Jade encouraged him to go back to the nine-year-old boy he was, full of dreams. He told her that he had it all before, "I had cars, a girlfriend, a kid and then I started using drugs being too clever with my own ideas, having too much money. I didn't have to worry about money and I ended up with nothing. I had it all." The tape picked up his frequent yawning, but he seemed to relate very well and opened up to her. It was quite astonishing how she read him so well and pierced his soul. She used Tarot cards and turned over the Magician card foretelling his taking control of his life. The last card was the Sun card which she said signified better things. "This year needs to be a whole new journey. You don't know what's around the corner but it's positive. It's a journey that you don't know what's going to happen. But here is the card of pleasure."

She discussed his failures and turned them into positive lessons for the future and spoke at length about his role as a father and how he should take pride in his daughter and that she should be proud of him. She foretold better things were on the way. She promised he would attract the new woman he desired if he cultivated a new positive energy. She patiently explained to him by slowing down, keeping steady, he would get there. She ended the sitting by emphasizing his strengths, as to how good he was at creating things with his hands.

Henry left the reading elated. But the feeling didn't last long. With nothing to do and nowhere to go, he continued on his downhill spiral. Despite Jade's best efforts, Henry could not apply himself or see anything through without constant supervision. He even lacked the motivation to go fishing or otherwise spend time in nature on his own. Ultimately, he was comfortable only with familiarity. Desperate, he visited the Hostel, only to be turned away. With no other options, he checked into hospital, where his psychiatrist promptly discharged him.

I took Henry to a Salvation Army Sunday morning service. But Henry, painfully shy in unfamiliar surroundings, was not sociable or communicative. Interestingly, Henry was at his most open and honest that day. He acknowledged that he couldn't express or feel love, which he did not understand. He felt nothing, he said, even when I or others hugged him. He enjoyed sex but did not associate it with love. He had been so despairing that, several months ago, he laid down on the road in front of a pub, with no intention of getting up. He went uninjured only because someone pulled him to safety. "What's the point?" he asked. "It's always the same thing. A hand comes and pulls you up and then you fall down again. Up and down, up and down, like a yo-yo. I think many times I might just as well start fixing again, until the end comes."

Still undeterred, I encouraged Henry to attend the Army's second service and social events that afternoon and dropped him outside. I was quite pleased with myself when we parted: Henry would no longer have to walk the streets alone on Sundays. But Henry never did return to the Salvation Army. It wasn't him, he said. Still, he was happier, having chosen instead to visit his daughter at the home where she lived with her mother, her mother's partner, and their child. Henry hadn't laid eyes on his daughter for over a year, when a chance meeting on the street led to the renewal of their relationship. He loved showing her the places he and I had discovered on our many walks.

Henry's success had become a personal challenge for me, but I was running out of ideas, especially because there were signs aplenty that Henry was looping out of control yet again. Back on heroin, he had taken to calling me regularly, his moods unpredictable. At one point, Henry called me, absolutely irate and demanding I see him because he "couldn't speak on the phone." I agreed, largely because he was with George, a hostel resident I hadn't seen for many months. I was eager to know how George was doing.

It all culminated when an untaxed car that Henry kept on his mother's council estate wouldn't start. Henry asked me to help by pulling his car with a towrope tied to mine. I agreed in the hope that fixing the car would be a positive catalyst for him. We met at his mother's, timing it for when her partner, a postman, who spent his free time boozing and wouldn't allow Henry into his home, wasn't around. I arrived before Henry did, but his mother greeted me hospitably. A pretty woman despite her unruly hair, she worked as a cleaner and didn't have much to say, other than that she was glad Henry was no longer in trouble. Henry was agitated when he arrived. He couldn't sit still. And for the first time, he tried to put his arm around me. I moved away. Soon, we set out to start the car. On the way there, he moved toward me again. When I rejected him, he ran ahead, leaving the landing door to fall on me. Nonetheless, I made it to the car. It jerked to life twice but stopped almost as abruptly. On the third occasion, Henry roped his car to mine. I gave him a pull – to no avail. Henry got out of his car and kicked it with such force that it caused a great dent in the rear door. I tried to calm him, but he was in a rage. I knew that he could lose control and lash out at me at any moment. So I left. And that was our last encounter. I had lost the battle. Apart from passing Henry by car as he stood waiting for a bus, I never saw him again. Yet I often wonder what happened to him. Last I heard, he was taking meals at soup kitchens and had been "nicked" for shoplifting at an off-license. A few months later, though, I dreamt of Henry. It was a terrible dream: he was thin, homeless, sleeping rough, and wielding a knife. Instead of embracing him, as was my custom, I rode off on my bicycle, terrified that he was lurking about no matter where I went. When I awoke, I phoned his mobile. It was not in service.

Henry lost his hold on his life. He lacked values, self-respect and dignity. Unable to see a future, he couldn't rise above his present. He had given up. He should have stopped treating the meaning of life as if it were something external to him: he could only put meaning into his life and relieve his own suffering from within. Henry had to let the tears flow and deal with the present in the realization that he couldn't change the past. But Henry had decided not to be worthy of his suffering. In doing so, he lost what he needed most: the inner freedom to bear suffering meaningfully by taking advantage of his angst to realize his values and give his life meaning. His mental condition made it all impossible.

I had noticed Henry largely because he stood out from the other residents who were, for the most part, unkempt and bedraggled. Not only was he the best looking, but he also possessed a certain style the others lacked. It wasn't that he was the only one to sport a diamond-studded earring; overall, he was very clothes conscious and wore designer logo shirts hanging outside his trousers. He was over six feet tall with ginger-colored hair, gleaming green eyes, and a wonderful physique, albeit exceptionally slim. In other words, attractive.

It was only after many months working with him that I discovered that Henry had learning difficulties, a low I.Q., a psychopath with multiple personalities and an arsonist whose glittering eyes and stylish appearance were characteristic of his personality disorder. Like all psychopaths, he was extremely manipulative – and certainly managed to manipulate me. I knew, of course, that he had been to prison. But I never questioned him about it, and all he told me was that he had been incarcerated for drug-related offences. He also admitted, without being asked, to being a thief who stole tools from building sites. In the end, he was clever enough to offer information that would make his type of criminality a lesser form of evil. He knew how to gain my confidence and gave me no reason to doubt him. Hindsight tells me that I should have been on my guard, less starry-eyed, and less intent on saving the world single-handedly. But then this story would have ended before it began.

The psychological profile of a psychopath describes an individual who lacks emotion or conscience, cannot love or fear, and seeks self-gratification at anyone's expense. He is often glib and superficial; a clever conversationalist who reads body language well. He is also slightly autistic, egocentric, grandiose and has a strong sense of entitlement. Most psychopaths have a traumatic birth or childhood. They don't get along with others, but somehow make a good impression. Behind it all is a lack of remorse or guilt. Psychopaths lack empathy, are deceitful and manipulative, and have shallow emotions. The lack of emotion creates a great need for stimulation or excitement that will provide the "kicks" that normal emotions might provide to others. They live by their own rules, espousing wonderful plans and grandiose ideas – with no idea on how to act on them. Psychopaths rationalize their behavior, even to the point where they might feel justified in killing someone who is laughing at them. Unable to feel others' pain, they are indifferent to suffering, so much so that they can be exceptionally cruel to animals. Family members are merely possessions. Psychopaths are also very irritable, highly resistant to discipline and oversensitive to perceived insults. Psychopathy is incurable and untreatable.

Only after I knew Henry for a long time did I realize how serious were his problems. At the outset, his rage and violence were likely in remission, perhaps because of the excitement of the new "relationship" with me. And it wasn't just the idea of having someone new in his life, it was having someone who cared, temporarily filling a void in a boring, meaningless existence. To make matters worse, I fed his feelings of grandeur and being special by constantly praising, listening, and caring. It was only when the stressors built up that Henry's true pathology emerged. At that point, he fell into such rage over a minor incident that he could barely restrain himself from hitting me. What then became clear was that I could not deal with Henry. My only choice was to cease contact immediately. I wasn't the first who had reached out, but like those before me, I had gone as far as I could. What he really needed was a full-time support system. When I cut off contact, he returned to his lonely existence and distorted thoughts, leaving him ill-equipped to cope with the real world. I still remember that when I asked him to jot down his feelings, he scrawled, "I vil emt" – as in "I feel empty and alone."

I was advised not to have anything more to do with Henry and ease myself out of the relationship without letting him know. I was given a phone number to call in case I needed help. The situation had become dangerous and out of hand because he was calling me persistently, insisting that he had to see me in person. One night he called me six times, until I finally turned off my phone. The next day he apologized, saying he'd been drunk – but I knew that wasn't the case at all. In the end, I became truly afraid. With his history of arson in mind, I imagined he might turn up on my doorstep and torch my car. Other wild scenarios also plagued me. I took to driving up to my home cautiously, fearful that he might jump out from behind a bush. I never answered my phone, instead leaving the answering machine on.

When Henry finally got me on the line, I explained how my life had changed. I had other preoccupations and relationships. Knowing that it would put him off, I rattled on about spirit and God until he rang off on the pretext that nature was calling. The next time he phoned, I followed the same formula. He lost patience, and I never heard from him again.

Chapter Eight

Life in a Nursing Home

When there is love between two people, they can stand together on the head of a pin. When there is hate, the whole world is not wide enough for them to coexist.
—Ibn Gabirol

I always hoped that Gloria wouldn't sit anywhere near the exercise class. Her voice carried and she wouldn't stop talking about the minutiae of her 90 years of family life. Her mind had gone only in the last year or so. But I took notice only when I realized she was sinking ever more deeply into a world of silence. I wished she would come to life again so that I could cherish her distraction. Seeing her sitting as in outer space, suddenly looking very old and feeble, shrinking a few inches as she withdrew further from reality, was a much worse alternative.

The majority I encountered in these homes were in their twilight years. To be sure, a handful of younger people who could not care for themselves and had nowhere else to go were also part of the tapestry. Their commonality was their disability, be it age-related, genetic, or episodic. As James Hollis, the American Psychoanalyst said, as they decline, people become more of what they already were: "Those who whine now will whine more; those dependent now will become children; those in denial now will blame others; those who neglected growing up and assuming full responsibility for their emotional well-being will expect you to carry it when their powers decline. Double-burdened midlife adults, however functional they may be in other parts of their lives, will find it especially difficult to find a healthy balance." Worst of all, perhaps, most were resentful, unable to accept or resign themselves to their circumstances.

Although their spirit was in no position to thrive, many found temporary refuge in my class. I never had a lesson plan, but I did tend to follow the same pattern each week. The music I chose was my guide. I arrived intending to give 100 percent of myself. I regarded each class as a challenge. I prided myself on my ability to get the most recalcitrant of people moving, to turn people who vegetated all week into active, happy individuals, albeit temporarily.

Monday mornings took me to two large residential nursing homes in East London. The furnishings in the first were sparse. The front doors opened to an entrance lobby where sat those in the group who preferred not to associate with others. One man was propped up in a wheelchair, a blanket covering the space where his amputated legs should have been. The others, though gathered around him, were grumpy and dozy. Another individual who was well into his nineties seemed quite independent and mobile, but his worn clothes stained with food gave him away. Also in the group were a married couple who stayed close to each other, as well as some unshaven, bad-tempered old men. Yet another woman came and went as if walking in her sleep, not knowing quite where she belonged. This area led into a large open plan lounge/dining area. It featured a "breakfast bar" to which staff passed food from an adjoining noisy kitchen. The absence of carpeting contributed to the noise that resulted from diners constantly dropping things. I always arrived after breakfast. By then, staff had washed the floor and mounted plastic notice board warnings against walking on the slippery surfaces. At one end were simple, uncushioned dining chairs and tables. After meals, residents were moved a few feet to comfortable chairs that faced each other in something approximating a half-circle. The second home I visited on Monday mornings had the same management and was very similar in arrangement and décor. Indeed, few of the homes I visited were welcoming or warm. Body odor and the smell of fluids pervaded some. The floors had to be washed daily, so they were rarely carpeted, leaving bare surfaces that amplified the screeches and other dissonant sounds made by metal trolleys, walking frames, stainless steel cutlery, and thick plates and cups that either traversed or fell on them.

Although the 22 classes I conducted each week were quite diverse, there were many similarities. The people in the luxury residences had the same problems and characteristics as those in poorer, more austere environments. With one exception, the television was always on. Residents clutched tabloid newspapers that they barely read. Others dozed. Staff was constantly taking someone to the toilet. To be sure, the poorer homes were the ones that reeked of urine, feces or over-exuberantly sprayed room freshener. Life, it seemed, revolved around meals and tea. Almost everyone, bored and lacking motivation, was tired. Many residents believed themselves to be above their neighbors and so rarely ventured from their rooms. Some, who had fallen on hard times, looked like they belonged in more refined surroundings, like fish out of water.

The death of a spouse of many years is deeply traumatic for the survivor of even an unhappy marriage. The body rhythms of partners synchronize, and they fire off each other's energies. Learning to depend on ourselves without leaning on others, however, is an opportunity for enormous actualization that can validate our existence in our twilight years. We all have undiscovered talents that go to the grave with us. Certainly, it's easier to mourn than to find the inner strength that sees loss as a new starting point for self-awareness and self-love. But there are opportunities to, for example, enjoy the fruits of one's labor or marvel at the children and grandchildren who are our progeny. Individuals who dote on wasted lives and wallow in regret live in awareness of their failures to the bitter end. What really surprised me was how often I heard people saying they didn't want to live any longer, as if every year after 70 was one year too many. Almost daily, I overheard someone wishing themselves dead. No wonder they presented as old people: they had lost the will to live. Still, the many who bounced back after they became ill amazed me; I had written most off. But no matter how frail and devoid of hope these individuals had appeared, they found something to hold on to and fight back. Was it the fear of death, or are we just meant to hang in there until our turn comes? I particularly remember a 94-year-old woman who had recently had a stroke. She'd been starving herself for so long it seemed reasonable to assume the stroke would finish her off. The will to go on had originally left her 12 years previously, when her only son died. Her grandchildren, busy with their large families, had no time for her, leaving her alone for the most part. Practically blind and stuck in a seemingly meaningless life, she managed, nonetheless, to go on and on.

One home that stood out from the rest housed sophisticated, independent older people who didn't suffer from incontinence. The home was luxurious, with marble floors and high decorative standards. The lounge featured comfortable couches and period chairs that gave it the air of a smart country home. Everyone, including the uniformed staff, was well turned out. But as soon as residents could no longer fend for themselves, management moved them to a nursing facility run by the same company. The owners were a doctor and wife team, and a son who joined them as their profitability grew. Their overriding interest was in profit, without pretensions of caring or altruism. Greed was all over their faces. Privately, they were contemptuous of their charges. Yet it was the most expensive home I encountered, provided the best service, and was soon completely full. No smells, no noise, no waiting for snacks or meals to arrive. Are grannies who live with their families any happier? Does a primitive instinct make us believe that a tribe should look after us? What I did notice, however, apart from their general humorlessness, was the residents' anger. Many could not reconcile themselves to their institutionalization. Some felt abandoned by families who could have taken them into large homes. There is, after all, a saying that rings of truth: "A mother can have ten children, but one child cannot even look after one parent."

I was surprised to see Molly arrive with her sons at one of the retirement homes where I worked. I had met them just the weekend before at a friend's place. Molly, an elegant woman in her eighties, had emigrated from Australia, where she had a comfortable existence in the belief she'd be better off living close by her only son, a professional and empty nester with a large suburban home. His wife, a social worker, also worked from home.

But aside from being conveniently situated for family visits, the home offered Molly little.

She was like a fish out of water, an independent woman in good health surrounded by people who were not nearly as socially sophisticated. To make matters worse, this particular retirement home was utilitarian. Most of the residents were in poor health, including some suffering with dementia and Alzheimer's. The few women there with whom Molly might have enjoyed a worthwhile relationship were mobility-impaired and depressed. Poor Molly didn't have a chance. During her first week at the home, I found Molly sitting in a small, dark room frequented by women who were obviously bent on isolation. After breakfast, they went to the room, sank into their chairs, and soon fell sleep. Still, Molly obviously preferred their company to being alone, and so she joined them. I made a point of seeing Molly every week, but my attempts to entice her to my class failed. Instead, I watched her deteriorate rapidly. In the beginning, she did knit. Soon afterward, however, she began complaining of ill health. Before long, she was asleep in her chair like the others – a broken woman in ill health who looked 10 years older than when she arrived. What could Molly have done differently to keep her spirits up and remain the dignified, intelligent woman she was? What would I have done? I had little doubt that, similarly confronted with the pain of abandonment, my descent would have been as rapid and as steep.

Another private up-market nursing home I attended took on residents for whom the state paid. One such person was Dorothy, who babbled endlessly and loudly in the lounge, a constant intrusion on the peace and tranquility of those around her. She interfered with my class to the point that, on one occasion, I had her moved elsewhere.

We are all born with self-preserving, primitive emotions such as fear, anger, jealousy, envy, and greed. As people become more sophisticated and enlightened, they realize these emotions can be counterproductive. Yet many of the elderly continue to exhibit these negative feelings. It is true that older people lose millions of brain cells, but dendrites, or nerve connections, increase proportionately – the physiological basis for "older and wiser." So what's the difference between those of the elderly who thrive and those who don't. The best answer I know is in this bit of wisdom offered up by the authors of the Okinawa Way. "My conclusion is that some centenarians find their strength in God, some in their families, but many find it in the joy of living—in tasting an egg after going through years of war and famine when they could only dream of eggs, or simply drinking a glass of wine."

Chapter Nine

The Body – a barometer of life

Modern body building is ritual, religion, sport, art and science,
awash in Western chemistry and mathematics. Defying nature, it
surpasses it.
—Camille Paglia, 1992

The body is a barometer. It denotes and dictates the temperature of life. Nausea or revulsion, for example, are instincts the body uses to let us know that things aren't right – that the body, mind and spirit are not resonating. We've all heard the expression, "carrying the weight of the world on your shoulders," a reference to the stresses we hold in our bodies, stagnating its energy. We need something to remove the blockages. And this is where the mind comes in: simply talking and vocalizing can remove the obstructions. Anticipation and excitement indicate we're on the right track.

In the 1950s, heart disease, cancer, cirrhosis of the liver, accidents, influenza, pneumonia, car crashes, suicide, and homicide were the principle causes of death in people between the ages of 25 and 50. As many of these causes were linked to human behavior, they became the "barometer of these people's lives." In part, they stemmed from an inability to adjust to loneliness. Indeed, the loss of love, or never having had it, are contributing factors to the immune system's breakdown. Similarly, stress inhibits white blood cell receptors' ability to fight disease. A four-year study on nearly 1,000 middle-aged men found that hopelessness, failure or uncertainty about the future were linked with speedier onset of atherosclerosis. Using ultrasound, doctors concluded that hopelessness could be as harmful to the heart as smoking a pack of cigarettes daily. For their part, alcohol addiction and smoking cigarettes may result from an individual's lack of wholeness, in the sense that mind, body and spirit are not in harmony. When they are, we are on an even keel with the right chemical balance. There are fewer freak accidents because people who are whole have what it takes to control most events. Consider the proven correlation between speaking quickly and high blood pressure, which can be responsible for heart attacks. The mind of someone who speaks quickly is firing rapidly, affecting both the spirit and the body.

Human beings, regardless of color or shape, are alike. According to molecular biologists, we emerged some 40,000 to 50,000 years ago from a core group of no more than 10,000 women, who themselves originated in a small region of Africa about 100,000 years ago. There are some, like Richard Dawkins, who posit that our bodies are really machines blindly programmed by selfish genes and similar hardware. But many others, including biologist Stephen Rose, maintain that we are free agents, whose freedom rests in our molecules' interaction, a process governed by environmental as well as genetic factors. The result is the sum total of our experiences which, with the benefit of memory, endure. Our muscles are also memory banks for our emotions. The brain sends signals to them, and they respond by tensing. After a while, the responses become autonomic, no longer dependent on the signal from the brain to generate the response. It's all so inextricably intertwined that it brings to mind Plato's admonition: "Don't try to heal the body until you've healed the mind."

A child trained in ballet during its formative years learns to move visually, and instinctively holds himself erect. I only began ballet classes at 29, when my learning, now limited by psychological boundaries, was no longer so instinctive. My thought process had to become more visual. I had to concentrate and focus my attention on the rhythm. For me, the movements were not just exercises or dances, but a mind, body, and spirit experience. On the other hand, a ballet dancer, wife of a world-famous star, who had developed her visual brain from childhood, struggled academically. There are, however, laws of movement that apply to all people, of all ages, shapes and sizes. Carefully observed, they transport conscious movements into the subconscious, where they affect everyday life. The process instills control and order in the mind and fashions the way we treat the space around us. Freud said that "Emotional life and physical behavior correlate and work in unison." It follows that changing our physical patterns of behavior, our actions and our movements – through controlled movements to music, quiet controlled meditative energy flow in our body, our everyday activities, or through dance – our spontaneous subconscious interaction with the world and people around us changes too.

The first noticeable change I observed in my students was their growing confidence. Although developing confidence is both subconscious and is gradual, confidence does come with knowledge: knowledge, in turn, paves the route to control. As control demands dedication, determination and discipline – the very characteristics dance and exercise classes instill, practitioners feel and look better.

Ballet classes are based on biological and anatomical knowledge of the body coupled with safe standards of teaching exercises. Dance classes that incorporate the fundamental theories of Tai-chi, Yoga, Laban, Feldenkrais and the aural techniques of classical jazz and modern dance should be a challenging and satisfying experience for all. They expand personality, personal growth, and confidence. The objective is not only to produce professional dancers, but to provide opportunities for all to participate, enjoy and develop their talent and abilities to the extent they are able and find satisfying. The more one learns to believe in oneself – which dancing under proper and caring supervision encourages – the healthier one becomes. An understanding and working knowledge of the principles of correct body usage and dance technique are required, however, to achieve a rewarding level of execution – to make the body do what you want it to do! Simultaneously, the mind-body control that comes from knowledge, planning, and organizing movements must attend these principles. The real enjoyment of movement mastery, the exciting experience of dancing at any level does not emerge from mechanical routines, repetitive physical jerks, or mindless body movements. Undisciplined exercise in large classes, where financial gain is often the main objective, does not work. Proper dance training improves the body's immune system and can reduce illness from a range of causes.

A morning prayer in the Hebrew prayer book reads: "In wisdom thou has formed man, creating within him innumerable channels and many cavities, in Thy sublimity Thou knowest that if but one of them were to be ruptured or but one of them were to be blocked, it would be impossible to survive or subsist even for a short while." Many cultures believe in the invisible energy or force to which this morning prayer refers. But this energy must flow properly, and to achieve that, certain principles must govern. For example, it is difficult to exercise properly unless the body is relaxed. Maintaining good posture, correct alignment, and proper breathing technique, are all essential. It's important to remember, as well, that all movement begins from the center of the body. When all the muscles are engaged, there is a dynamic tension; when they are not, tension accompanies every action. The mind should be focused. Each movement must follow through as far as it can go, from the fingertips through the toes, allowing the energy to flow freely.

I'm often surprised by the way some people exercise. They think that they can do an exercise in whatever manner they choose. But you can't exercise one part of the body at the expense of others: one must always be mindful of the effect of a particular exercise on the rest of the body and the flow of energy. There are different types of exercise for different muscle activity. When exercise is of low intensity but of long duration, like long-distance running and swimming, it changes the muscle chemistry, leading to an increase in endurance with a minimum of fatigue. Endurance exercises produce changes not only in skeletal muscles but also in the respiratory and circulatory systems that improve the delivery of oxygen and fuel to muscles. In contrast, short duration, high intensity exercise – like weight lifting – increases muscle size, creating more power at the expense of endurance. It follows that we must choose exercises that are compatible with the activities we desire. As we age, intensity and duration of exercise will produce less change than in a younger person.

Our bodies have evolved ways of coping with fear and stress. We describe people who are angry as holding their stress in their jaw; inflexible people as stiff-necked; individuals experiencing fear as having tense shoulders; and the back as the bearer of financial insecurity burdens. Emotion is stored in the stomach; expressions like "butterflies in the stomach" refer to the way we feel when we're nervous. That is why this book is not just about the body or just about the mind. It is about the whole person and all the different aspects of the self that contribute to meaningfulness and purpose in life. Letting go, therefore, demands absolute relaxation of tension. By contrast, constipation holds onto waste and toxins that serve no purpose and run counter to our health. The enormous release that comes with elimination is both satisfying and relaxing; similarly, a sweating body is letting go. Sneezing, blowing the nose and cleaning the ears are also functions that rid of waste. Elimination of body waste, then, is tantamount to renewal.

Learning to let go of all tension in the mind and body is the goal. Allowing thoughts to twist and turn causes anxiety, stress and tension. The antidote is in working with your wisdom. Speak to it and ask the question: the answer will likely come when you are empty and open and expect it least. The body is constantly in flux, mimicking a fundamental law of nature that sees proteins, molecules and neurons interacting and reorganizing themselves constantly. When the demand for energy is greater than the immediate supply, the body tires. Each movement should use only the energy required for the task. It's like running a car: if you drive at an even speed and slowdown gently, you use less fuel. Driving mindfully creates less wear on the driver and the car. Similarly, using our energy intelligently and economically saves wear and tear on the body and mind.

I was an exercise therapist for the elderly, those with disabilities, "exceptionals" with special needs, and individuals with psychiatric and learning difficulties – all from different backgrounds. Some, in wheelchairs, were housed with others at different stages of dementia and mobile adults from 60 to 104 years of age. It made no difference to my classes. The exercises and the bodies were basically the same; only the limitations varied. After all, elderly people with neuro-disabilities have the same body structure as Rudolf Nureyev and Margot Fonteyn. The body is the finest instrument around. Played with respect and understanding, it can create a symphony united in an integrated whole. Fancy words, to be sure, but what do they mean? We are all made up of many thoughts and many personas: different masks for different tasks. The body speaks in the language of the environment that an individual encounters at any moment in time. When tense, the body becomes rigid in places. Relaxed, it opens up and unwittingly expresses itself in accordance with our moods. If a person is totally in tune with himself, he or she doesn't need different postures, because one – the right one – will do. Achieve happiness and inner contentment means being centered and whole, loving yourself and your body, and abandoning the ego. When all this is in place, everything works and moves together as it should. But if all this is so natural, why do we have to learn how to hold ourselves and how to move? It's because the way we live programs us and engineers our movements; it takes a lot of discipline to control the ego and the "shoulds."

The body is the only thing that you can trust. The mind tells us different things, but the body is truth. Sometimes we try to hide from or are unaware of our true feelings. When we repress certain feelings, like anger, we may develop a rash, stiffness, pain, or worse. We cannot use our body efficiently and economically – which is to say, play the instrument correctly – unless we treat it with respect. Once, while in a power boat traveling at high speed, I was thrown across the lower cabin parallel to the ground and tossed about like a paper airplane. As I bounced up and down, I realized just how vulnerable our bodies were. I could have cracked bones or even snapped my neck. I held on to some cushions and wedged myself between a bench and table, where I continued to bounce around like a rubber ball. The body, although amazingly resilient, is also fragile and easily damaged. No wonder, then, that almost everyone succumbs to some form of arthritis or wear and tear to the joints: since the boat incident, my knee has never been the same.

Using our energy efficiently and economically requires an understanding of how the body moves best, and the relationship between weight transfer and gravity. Consider a young, healthy and flexible tree, bending every which way in a ferocious wind, but rarely snapping. By contrast, dry, stiff branches break off easily. A relaxed, well-nourished and properly used body, then, can function like the young sapling for a long time. The mind directs the body. The body must do exactly what the mind tells it to do. To move successfully is to know how you intend to move going forward. That creates flow, rather than staccato actions which don't work. The mind must, however, understand and prepare so the action becomes an unconscious act, executed without hesitation. If the mind is tense, the body will be stiff. Oxygen, the life force, calms the mind when inhaled deeply. Every part of the body needs oxygen. My individual students all responded uniquely. Some took longer, perhaps years, to come around. Their defense mechanism resisted anything new; it took time and familiarity to break down the pushback. For some, anger was the only way they could communicate. I took it all as a challenge. Generally, my classes were successful and popular, even in summer, when the activity brought joy to their bodies and minds despite the heat. How was I able to work with so many people of such diverse abilities simultaneously? Some were quite capable of running around the room; others were partially paralyzed. On occasion, even the younger caregivers joined in. Everyone eventually responds to caring, and of course, the music that accompanied the class was, as most music is, magnetic.

The secret to physical grace is good posture. It doesn't matter what we wear or how tall we are. It's all about poise – how you hold yourself. Lift the spine from its base to the top of your ears, relax your body and pull it up with shoulders hanging loose, shoulder blades back and down, and let the weight of your hands tug at you. Think of the head separate from the neck, the neck separate from the shoulders. Straightening our spine straightens our emotional posture, albeit temporarily. So immediately gratifying was proper posture that it was one of the "tricks" I used to get people to join my classes. Conversely, holding parts of our body too tightly – due to fear, for example – can cause injury, as fear causes tension and constricts blood supply. In some personalities, heart attacks and strokes can occur; in others, extended repression of hurt or pain can cause cancer years later.

When he was 23, my brother, Claude, was diagnosed with lung cancer. Over radiation for a growth on his back 20 years earlier, which left him with mottled scarring, was probably the cause. Doctors gave him six months to two years. But after the lung was surgically removed, he enjoyed another 11 active years of life. To be sure, he fell ill from time to time. The last straw, however, may have been the depression caused by the dissolution of his marriage after just two years. The cancer returned and he died shortly after. Would he have lived longer in a happier marriage?

My father lived for exactly one year after Claude's death. It was just long enough to fulfill the duty to say Kaddish, the Jewish prayer for the dead that mourners repeat thrice daily for 11 months. Grief stricken and guilt-ridden over allowing Claude to be radiated, he quickly lost the will to live. Interestingly, scientists have identified a small spot on the brain, the insular cortex, as the possible center of extreme despair and consequent heart damage.

Happiness is the ability to be in control of your life. When I gave a talk on "Tips for a healthy and happy life," it came down to one sentence: "stay in control because it creates the ability to change behavior that is not conducive to a peaceful life." Understand how the body and mind interface, and be aware of your power to fashion internal happiness, regardless of the weather outside. But we have to be clear on what it is we want. If we want happiness, we won't find it. Wanting will never fulfill us because as soon as we have what we want, we won't be content. And eternal ecstasy never comes in material form. It comes from being the best person one can be and from realizing that we are here to serve. These realizations actualize our full potential and allow us to make the most of our innate talents.

A friend of mine, a high-powered, successful businesswoman, who had been divorced for many years, met a wonderful man also in his sixties. Eventually they married and moved abroad to a warmer climate. When I visited her there, she was distraught, involved in litigation with the building managers at their magnificent penthouse apartment. She had developed her rooftop terrace without permission and was not allowed to use it. As she saw it, she had been robbed of her dream. But a year later, when we met again, I found her a much more humble, human person. Although the problem hadn't been resolved, she had changed her attitude; having taken to counting her blessings, she had become a happier, better person.

I left my family at age 19 and moved from New York to London. In the late sixties, telephone calls were expensive and there was no email. When I couldn't sleep at night, I worried myself sick about my parents. It did nothing to help them, and they were getting on fine without me. But I did make myself terribly unhappy. So I decided not to worry, as it had achieved nothing. I practiced being in the moment and never thinking what would be, just what is. I taught myself to deal with reality and facts, blocking out the "what ifs."

I see the body as energy, a mass of vibrations. If we are low, we vibrate on a lower note than when we are content. The body stores energy at its center, and the energy's movement through the body that allows it to vibrate. When it flows, we are relaxed and lengthened; when we are tense, the tension blocks the energy, and our muscles shorten. I remember watching the ballet star Mikhail Baryshnikov dancing. I barely recognized his pirouettes, which he kept so tight and close to his center. That is what being strong is about. The greatest dancers are the most flexible and sensitive, but what sustains them is their ability to stay in control. Put another way, the body is a dynamic force of tension with every action having a reaction.

Here, then, are some techniques to maximize energy flow: The spine is the backbone and should be uplifted at all times, thus working most of the muscles. Lifting is the action of the head rising up and the feet pulling in the opposite direction. When we sit, pressure should be on our sitz bones, or bottoms, to maintain this pull, which should become as unconscious to us as is the force of gravity in holding the body upright. The world-famous Estonian dancer Thomas Edur told me that a properly held spine should create a firm, steely sensation. Donna Eden, a foremost advocate of energy healing and energy medicine, teaches her students to make changes and corrections by entering the body and manipulating meridians and energy flow. Her techniques visualize this energy system, which allows her to offer a practical guide to using it.

Where is the center of the body? Approximately two inches below the navel and halfway in. It corresponds to the middle of the sacrum, the only part of the body, aside from the skull, that doesn't move. It lies at the base of the spine and is composed of five fused vertebrae that form the body's strongest part. Some claim that the center of the body is also the center of understanding and wisdom. We all need a crutch, a place to go in times of need. Internally, this place is our center. It is the place where the sun always shines without regard to the external weather of our lives. If you sit comfortably, relax, close your eyes, and focus on this sanctuary, you can nourish the spirit and escape the now. This is meditation, which is about nourishing the spirit. The spirit, some say, itself has needs, including the need to go back from whence it came. Eastern religions and many spiritualists believe that, during meditation, the spirit leaves the body, returning to the spirit family for replenishment. That may certainly be the case: thousands of scientific studies, after all, recommend the practice. Indeed, yoga, meditation and other aspects of eastern religions and ritual have enticed many Westerners. One reason may be that, unlike the Christian world view, the Eastern perspective embraces the body as well as the mind. Learning Yoga – which means "union" – and its poses properly, for example, requires immersion in the philosophy and spiritual message behind the practice. Tai chi and the martial arts have a like foundation. Similarly, dancing professionally requires an understanding of the body as a whole and how it works with the mind if we are to achieve the control and precision of movement required.

The center of gravity alters when the body moves. For example, bending our knees leaves our center of gravity lower than when we're walking or jumping; to be in complete control, we must compensate by lifting the abdomen. Deep breathing is critical to maintaining control. It involves taking air in from the nostrils and pushing the diaphragm down so as to expand our lungs to their capacity; then holding onto the breath and releasing it slowly. Proper breathing allows all systems to function at full capacity and control. Here, then, are some further tips for exercising in a way that will help achieve full capacity and control.

Stretching

Stretching exercises begin from the center of the body and stretch from the end of the furthest point. If you're stretching up, dropping your hand, lead with the wrist, and let the fingertips do the pulling and lifting, allowing the energy to flow through a shoulder which is fully relaxed. Executed in this way, the stretch comes right through the arm and shoulder, running down the side of the body, all the way to the foot. Allow every stretch to be a full one – from top to toe. I can never forget the girl with a beautiful figure and massive muscular thighs. She made the mistake of pumping her thighs instead of lengthening from the toes when she did leg raises.

Bands

If you work with bands, pull at each end, not in the middle. It's the same principle with the body. If you crook your arm, lead with the elbow; if you bend at the knee, lead with the knee. If you want to work your inner thigh you might work through the heel – always from the furthest point. When leading with the fingertips, push a little further with the base of the palm; leading with the toe, you get more thrust by engaging the heel. Pull up your entire body as well as the muscles of the center. Engaging the abdominal muscles creates a more solid foundation that relieves pressure in other parts of the body.

Bending

Remember how the body is constructed: the joints are there precisely to facilitate bending. Bend from the hip joint, not from the middle of your back. Any exercise that involves bending forward means first elongating the back with the head pulling it up and then over at the hip joint. Backbends are different. To bend backwards, lift your head to elongate the spine, then lift your chest up, leading with it over backwards. Similarly, when you bend from the neck, the top of the head – the furthest point – leads. So it is when stretching with fingers or wrists: first the wrist, then the fingertips, encouraging the feel of working through our bones.

Building Muscle

To build muscles, you must shorten and tense them to block energy flow. You must isolate the muscle group that you want to build. The most efficient way to build muscle is from the center, by shortening the muscle fibers inward. The best way to take pressure off the joints is by strengthening the surrounding muscle groups. Working the muscle just above and around the kneecap, the patella, protects the knee. Weights are helpful, but not necessary: we can use our body weight to achieve a similar result. It takes fifteen pounds of resistance to build muscle. This can easily be achieved by pushing the toes or heel against the floor while working the muscle above the knee. The same can be done for the calf muscle by pushing on your toes and using your body weight whilst shortening muscle. It's essential to squeeze the muscles: never jerk them. All the muscles of the body can be worked by this same method: isolating, foreshortening and using body weight for resistance.

Balance

To be fully anchored, our weight should be distributed evenly with the belly button between the feet. To balance on one foot, the belly button must move over the ball of the supporting foot, which is holding all the weight. Contract the gluteal muscle (under the buttocks) of the supporting leg, to give greater strength, support and hold. Again, you must involve the abdominal muscles. Do not use your entire body because it will tire easily, and you will perspire unless your muscles are already strong. Holding the unweighted leg in position allows you to maintain your balance for longer; also, moving the unweighted leg makes it impossible to tense the gluteal muscle. Energy must flow through both sides. When rising from a chair or from the floor, take the body weight forward and up: the dynamics will carry you in the same way an airplane takes off, to let the dynamics carry you like an airplane.

Remember also that music, which lifts the spirit is a wonderful medium for exercising: the body becomes the instrument that sings to the tune. Whenever I turned on the music in a nursing home, people who looked dead in their chairs came alive.

Exercise apart, there are other ways to nourish the spirit. Prayer can be beneficial, keeping in mind that it is there for the benefit of the individual, not for God. When life is difficult or painful and there aren't any answers, prayer is often the last resort. It's not necessary to take a long time in prayer or meditation: a few minutes is often quite enough. While many speak of "emptying the mind," it's really more about clarity and focus. Prayer places you in equilibrium, the spiritual equivalent of the body's center, the place where you find balance.

Gratitude, often incorporated in prayer, can be a very important exercise. Those who regularly give thanks for all they have, accept their situation whatever it might be, allow themselves to learn, grow and get in touch with themselves, usually have better lives.

There is a prayer of thanks about which it is said that "whoever recites the prayer turns severe judgements into mercy and merits outright miracles from the Creator." It is a prayer than many cultures can embrace. I commend it and reproduce it in full:

Thank you (the name), King of Kings and Master of the World! Thank you for the infinite times that you helped me, supported me, rescued me, encouraged me, cured me, guarded over me and made me happy. Thank you for always being with me. Thank you for giving me the strength to observe Your commandments, to do good deeds and pray. Thank You for all the times You helped me, and I didn't know how to say, "Thank you." Thank you for all the loving kindnesses you do for me each and every moment. Thank You for every breath I breathe. Thank You (the name) for all the things that I do have and thank you (the name) even for the things that I don't have. Thank You for my periodic difficulties, my occasional setbacks and for the times when I don't feel happy, because everything is for my ultimate benefit, even if I don't see that it's always for my best. Deep in my heart, I know that everything that comes from You is the very best for me and designed especially for me in precision and exacting Divine Providence of which only the King of Kings is capable. Thank you for the periodic times that are difficult for me, for only that way do they enable me to fully appreciate the good times, for only after being in darkness one can appreciate the light. Thank You for the wonderful life You have given me. Thank You for every little thing that I have, for everything comes from You and from no one else. Thank You for always listening to my prayers. Creator of the World, I apologize from the bottom of my heart for all the times that I didn't appreciate what You gave me and instead of thinking of You, I only complained. I am dust and ashes, and You are the entire universe. Please don't ever cast me away. (CKLfoundation@aol.com)

Silence is also a powerful medium. It allows you to escape into yourself so that you can see and hear more clearly the ambient vibrations that you don't pick up when you are too engrossed in the external. Too much silence, however, can be deafening. It's a matter of being open to the sounds and sights around us: that's what becoming clairaudient or clairvoyant is all about. Occupied minds cause us to lose sensitivity to our surroundings. Thoughts float to the surface only when the body is relaxed, and the mind focused on emptiness. The emptier and more open you can be, the more likely it is that you will experience real wisdom and free memories and insights – even those of which you may be unaware.

We can also increase our creativity by encouraging the unconscious. Henri Poincare, the nineteenth-century French mathematician, spent six months contemplating a particular problem, but the answers came to him only as he got on a bus. But much as we might want, we cannot be allowed to hear the "Voice" at all times. If we could, we would lose our freedom to choose. A world in which the "Voice" is constantly heard does not challenge its population. Creation called for a world of Divine silence, in which we can uncover the "Concealed Voice" — which each of us has heard somewhere and at some point, however fleetingly.

Many people are without direction, fragmented, all over the place, unrounded and not centered. They fire on all fronts. But they can use their body to control their life because the body's center is the temple of the soul. Learning to come home to oneself and to return to that home can be a source of strength and comfort. Before we can find our center, however, we must find our feet. A good way to achieve this is by closing our eyes and visualizing ourselves as an elephant taking slow deliberate steps, sinking into the ground as it gives under our weight. A popular alternative is reflexology, because our feet house the nerve endings of all our organs. Rooting and grounding provide a sense of security.

To understand the present, we must engage the past. Our evolutionary role is to have, feed, and protect children. We started as hunters and gatherers who often had a long way to go to find their sustenance. That's why bodies are meant to be active. Compare, for example, the running river that picks up momentum as it moves along, to the stagnant pond that clouds up as it fills with toxins. When we move, we increase our ability to move more, and so build up strength, stamina and release toxins. The less we move, the less able we become. The greatest inducement for exercise is that it preserves youth. Exercise improves how the heart and lungs function, lowers blood pressure, increases muscle strength, and improves bone density. It also enhances flexibility, reaction times and clarity of thought, even as it reduces susceptibility to depression, and retards and possibly reverses the effects of aging. By improving the quality of life, exercise prolongs it.

Many psychiatric ex-offenders were unable to engage in controlled exercise. They were so heavily drugged, so bereft of motivation, and so incapable of engagement, all indicative of a disconnect between mind and body. The upshot was they were out of touch with their feelings, which were often painful. To survive emotionally, they cut off part of themselves, making it impossible for them to relate to their bodies. To be sure, many could muscle-build mindlessly to stave off attacks and enhance their image and ability to intimidate. Fortunately, I worked in some psychiatric units where the residents were still a part of society and wanted to help themselves. There, I had more success.

This being said, my goals were the same for all my students: learn how to use the body efficiently and economically. If they did so, the elderly, for example, could learn enough control to minimize falls. I concentrated on making my students more aware of using their feet, which we tend to do less often as we age. I demonstrated exercises that helped focus their minds to make them more thoughtful in their movements and more alert. I encouraged control of the eyes and use of the center in distributing their weight. I tried to improve their mood, which helped them exercise greater control. I encouraged good posture, explaining that it would let them move their bodies with less effort. People with learning disabilities, however, were most challenging. They had difficulty remembering the techniques I taught them from one class to the next: each class seemed as if it was the first. The improvements that did take place rarely survived the day, forcing my disabled students to learn them all over again in the next class. As the severely brain damaged, sometimes referred to as "those people who speak with a silent prayer," I could only hope that they absorbed the love and energy I gave them.

The body is the barometer of life. I was weary at times, but physically stronger than ever from teaching four to five classes a day. My own dancing improved, and every day was rewarding. I took comfort in knowing that I was responsible for giving, but it was up to the students to be willing to receive. Frequently, I saw tremendous improvement in the way students performed: their posture improved momentarily, releasing the pressure on their organs; they were relaxed, focused, happy, had more stamina, their breathing improved, and their expressions changed

As the energy emerged, they came alive again. By exercising in a controlled, efficient and economical manner, they became the instruments of the music, and the music became food for their soul.

The body is the vehicle of the spirit. The spirit seeks harmony. If the mind is in turmoil and the body stressed, the soul is not at peace. The sputtering, strained engine cannot propel the vehicle beyond a certain point. The energy must flow through the body if the spirit is to exercise its power.

Chapter Ten

When Love Has Gone

Love is the ultimate goal to which man can aspire.
—Viktor Frankl

I remember once reading that only five percent of the population are any good at what they do. Unfortunately, few of the staff, administrators or residents at the four or five homes I attended each day qualified for inclusion in that group. That could make things difficult in my "new world" where anger, downright unpleasantness and aggression were so prevalent, and where residents spat at and kicked me. Still, they weren't wild animals, just deeply frustrated individuals. I always tried to respond with respect and kindness, and eventually won most of them over. There was the occasional failure, like the violent old boy in his nineties, who spat and threw things at anyone who came near him. He went ballistic when I intruded on his space by playing music and exercising nearby, making a habit of hobbling over to my tape recorder and trying to smash it up. Scuffles always followed when anyone tried to stop him. Then there were Judy and Mary, who persisted in shouting out at each other and making derogatory comments so loudly that it wasn't possible to run a class. It was the only time I requested assistance. But the following week, Judy and Mary sat quietly, taking things in somewhat sheepishly. People can change, but only if motivated. It is all about this ethereal thing we call energy. In a positive climate, positive energy will take over. Continually firing from the negative side of the brain reduces the positive side's capacity and it starts to deteriorate. "Use it or lose it" is really apt here.

Miss Bishop was one of the most interesting cases I came

across. A very slim woman in her eighties, you could still see the traits that must have made her an extremely attractive girl and woman. She was a German Jew. I'm still not sure whether she had a genetic predisposition to aggressive and abuse behavior or whether the origins of her conduct lay in her wartime experiences. Miss Bishop had spent most of her life in a psychiatric unit in England until she was transferred to the home for elderly psychiatric cases where I met her and where she stood out not only from the other residents, but from any of the residents in any of the homes I'd ever attended. An Asian couple owned this particular home where the wife took an active role. She didn't separate individual suffering from different conditions into discrete groups; rather, she herded all the residents into a single large lounge. The woman was annoying, petty and stupid. Her only topic of conversation with me focused on how to avoid wasting incontinence pads. She eventually reduced my class to every other week, with no regard for the benefits and enjoyment of the residents – who otherwise had to do with basic necessities – derived from the classes.

It took years for Miss Bishop to allow me to touch her. If anyone went near her, she jumped as panic crossed her face. When I finally did touch her, she cried "yuck" and complained about my allegedly clammy hands. For a time, she shouted abuse at me and called me names in German and English. And she hated men: whenever one came into the room, she invariably called him an asshole – but in German. Among Miss Bishop's targets was a very depressed man who slept in the corner of the room and watched television all day. He never spoke. His clothes were dirty and wrinkled, as if he had slept in them. His face featured a stubbly, grizzly-looking beard. When Miss Bishop was bored, a state easily achieved in this stimulus-free environment, she made vomiting-like sounds and called him every name under the sun. She particularly disliked anyone of color, including staff, and persisted in calling them names. In the process, she isolated the newest most vulnerable staff member whom she tormented with intense abuse. Miss Bishop also picked up on physical traits. If she caught people scratching their heads, she went on about how they were lice-infested. When her "super hate" of the week appeared, the wildcat in her emerged, growling as she flailed her talons. Many staff complained that she had scratched them. And she once hit an Alzheimer's patient who was nothing more than a vegetable.

But aggression, I had, discovered was a defense mechanism concealing a fearful, weak personality. So I never allowed Miss Bishop, or anyone else, to intimidate me. As they railed, I habitually stood close to them, taking care to appear confident but kind. It was against my nature to fight. Then one day, a girl in the ballet class I attended, came right into my space, blocking my movement. I bumped into her lightly during the sequence. When she hadn't budged to make way for the next spin, I pounded her with my arm and leg as I pirouetted. She was shocked but wouldn't move. So I shouted out, "If you don't get out of my space, I'll hit you again." She moved away. The incident pleased me because I was not naturally assertive – more likely passive aggressive.

Still, I always apologized if I had in fact upset them. At the start of one class, I turned a woman's chair around so that she could face the group. She had been sitting quietly, but suddenly burst out in a torrent of abuse. She told me how much she hated me and that she wanted neither myself nor my dancing. Later, staff explained that my intrusion had upset her psychological balance of space and peace. They were right: by lesson's end, she was fine again. The incident made me more aware of avoiding intrusiveness and being respectful of others' space. Regardless how nice we may appear to be, we all have our personal agenda. But no one can have free rein without being answerable for their actions. Indeed, free rein is more freedom than most people can cope with. The old lady in the chair was absolutely right: I had no business intruding on her space without her permission, inducing her into self-preservation mode.

A smidgen of respect and kindness, I had learned, went a long way to breaking down barriers. Self-discipline, in the form of fastidiousness, also helped. If everything around is in a disordered state, the eye takes it in, and the mind interprets it. So much so that some say you can always learn the state of a woman's mind by looking in her handbag. With this in mind, I trained myself to be orderly at all times, like arranging my shoes neatly side to side after I took them off. It made a difference, so much so that I even managed to win over Miss Bishop, who went so far as to admit that she liked me. Another woman eventually came round to apologize for her own behavior and soon evolved into a sweet and mellow personality. Patience was absolutely essential in dealing with these people. It was important not to react, but rather to transcend the situation and determine what was really happening. As it turned out, the lesson – respond, not react – proved valuable in many facets of life. Unfortunately, few of the staff I came across ever understood that there were almost always two sides to a story, especially with individuals as complex as the damaged residents they encountered. Few staff had the patience to go the extra mile. Still, I avoided doing too much as I had discovered that, to the extent they surrendered their powers to others, the residents tended to resign themselves to dependence. When people enter nursing facilities, they often relinquish their responsibilities to themselves and instead just hand themselves over to others. The most common problem I faced was an individual's reluctance to join in and do any movement. I had to use gentle persuasion and sometimes a bit of force: my philosophy was to bring them in kicking and screaming. Naturally, this offended the rules. But I never had a problem: the people I dragged in let me get away with it because they knew I cared. Once I got them going, they responded to the momentum. I often asked myself whether my efforts were worthwhile. What did an hour of movement really do for people who did nothing otherwise? My responsibility, I decided, was to do the best I could, which was to get them motivated and alert. They were ultimately responsible for their own health, so the rest was up to them.

Older people have a real or imagined need to go to the toilet frequently. It can become a habit, as their bladders become accustomed to frequent emptying. Many are incontinent and never accept the idea of using incontinence pads. Staff regularly punished frequent toilet-goers by ignoring them or leaving them on the toilet for too long. I had often seen the frequent goers ignored or punished by being left on the toilet, to teach them a lesson.

A case in point was Gregory, tall and attractive, who appeared much younger than his years and was clearly too young for the home. A stroke had incapacitated his left side. As he was on a high fiber supplement for constipation, his wheelchair was always close to the bathroom. On one occasion, however, an upset stomach mandated more frequent trips to the bathroom than usual. The caregiver's response was to leave him on the toilet, ignoring his protestations. To make matters worse, Gregory was difficult to understand because the stroke had also affected his speech. I could feel his frustration. As it turned out, Gregory's family had employed me to give him private lessons. A thrice married "bon vivant," his divorces had depleted the fortune he had made running a large company. Bad enough that life had dealt him a massive stroke in his youth, but to be treated like a naughty child at this stage of life was unfathomable. Later, I reported the incident to the family. But I didn't report it to the home: as I spent just an hour there weekly, reporting the incident would only have produced enmity and produced no positive impact on Gregory's life. This was especially so because the head of the home was a simple man and not an effective leader. Indeed, the environment in most homes took on the character of the person in charge. If he or she was in control, the demeaning behavior that Gregory experienced would have been a rare occurrence.

Loneliness, the lack or loss of love, or never having had it, is a major factor in physical, mental, and emotional decline. Adjusting to being alone is particularly difficult for people who have had constant partners, good or bad, for most of their adult lives. The heartache brought on by loneliness or otherwise contributes to the immune system's breakdown. So does the adjustment required when an individual starts a new life in a retirement or nursing home. For a time at least, confusion and fear abound.

I worked at a London nursing home for about 40 frail and immobile residents, a colorful assortment of characters, many of them mentally unstable. Most of their faces were etched with the signs of a hard, simple life, one that, as evidenced by their rough hands, probably involved manual labor. For the most part, they were far past their "sell by" dates, so much so that it shocked me, though I certainly didn't lack exposure to human degradation. The residents spent their days in their chairs. Staff rarely took them outside. Their simple rooms featured a bedside table, a chest of drawers, a small freestanding hanging wardrobe, a chair, and a sink. The floors were highly polished linoleum, and there were no private bathrooms. The curtains were unlined, allowing the early morning light to enter even when closed. Clinical, smelling of urine and reminiscent of a Victorian hospital is probably the best way to describe the place. The sister in charge was a large, kindly woman who always looked correct in her nursing uniform. She cared about her charges and imbued them with confidence that they were in good hands. What I didn't understand was how she could employ an absolute dragon as the senior assistant in charge of the residents' menial daily requirements. To be sure, that miserable woman had her favorites, whom she treated tenderly. But these favorites were invariably the residents who required the least attention. I was absolutely disgusted by the way she treated some of my students. Rude and aggressive, she treated them with contempt, a scowl always on her face. She delivered food as if she was throwing it at her charges. This was not a place of peace and calm. Commotion reigned as a result of the constant traffic to the toilet, occasional visitors, the bustle of shift changes, and the unrelenting background of metal pots and pans clicking and clacking against steel surfaces. There was no privacy, no personal dignity.

Carol, a scrawny, dark-haired woman who wore pilled skirts and sweaters as her habit, spent her days engrossed in imaginary conversations that sometimes bordered on the violent, punctuated by four letter expletives as part of imagined verbal fights and talk of prison. But no one took notice: she had become part of the background noise. Elizabeth was different. Mobile, healthy-looking, well-spoken, nicely turned out, wearing real jewelry and haughty with hair that hadn't yet all turned gray, she didn't belong among people who had no hope that life would get better and many of whom already had one foot in the grave. Elizabeth came from an independent living environment where she was free to move about, only to arrive in a place where humanity was at its most vulnerable. After the initial orientation, Elizabeth gravitated to Neeta, a stroke victim suffering from dementia. Elizabeth took it upon herself to demand that staff pander to Neeta's constant and unreasonable whims. For example, Neeta tended to slip into an uncomfortable position in the home's oversized chair, made of slippery vinyl. Elizabeth demanded that she be readjusted every ten minutes. Needless to say, Elizabeth was soon out of favor with staff. What was odd, however, was that Neeta and Elizabeth rarely spoke. Indeed, Neeta seemed something of a human pet for Elizabeth, someone she could love, attend, and fuss over. When

Neeta died, Elizabeth's grief was profound. With no one to take her pet's place, she became overly absorbed in her large handbag. Previously my most able and motivated student, she lost all interest in exercise, television or anything other than constantly opening her handbag, rummaging through it and withdrawing its contents to check that everything was there, and then closing it yet again. I now realized she suffered from obsessive-compulsive disorder. When Neeta died, Elizabeth's obsession transferred from a person to an object. Though she sat right in front of me, she never participated in the class again.

Maggie was another resident who kept to herself. She was in her sixties and seemed strong despite a heart condition. When not stressed, she was a diamond-in-the-rough with a kindly disposition. But she was also of quick temper, particularly when a co-resident, Rhona, repeatedly insisted on undressing in public to the point where she was totally naked. So persistent was Rhona that I, there for only an hour weekly, got to know every inch of Rhona's generous body. Clearly, she was histrionic and badly in need of attention. In fact, she attracted attention quite apart from the histrionics: she had learning disabilities, spoke in grunts and bore an expression on her heavy, stubbly face that clearly indicated that "the light was on but no one was home."

Loneliness gives rise to strange couplings. Rhona had been a regular source of irritation for Maggie, who made her disgust for the strip show evident and frequently reprimanded Rhona. Then something happened, and they became inseparable. Their relationship blossomed into love that fostered public demonstrations of affection. Suddenly, and apart from the occasional relapse, Rhona didn't undress anymore. She joined the exercise group, bringing joy and pride to Maggie. If Rhona so much as raised her leg or arm to do an exercise, Maggie was ecstatic. In this home where most lives ended, Rhona's began. Quietly holding hands with Maggie, she sat happily and fulfilled for hours.

Fear of falling was another universal problem I encountered in the elderly. Those who had led an active life combined with exercise had a better sense of their bodies and understood how to transfer their weight when moving. Rina, a volunteer with ballet training, was a fine example. In her nineties and older than most of the residents, she still walked wherever she could. Her trouser suits, wig, a modicum of makeup and a mentally alert affect made her look decades younger than she was. So it was as well with a 96-year-old gentleman whom I saw on social occasions at the home. He walked three miles daily and stayed out late nightly. He self-managed his complex financial affairs and read avidly. His hearing was his only discernible impairment. In the public eye, the Queen Mother, who reached her centenary, was another example of an elderly person who maintained a healthy, active lifestyle. Her daughter, the Queen, still rides horses at age 94 and is married to Prince Philip, who recently died at 99 years old. To be sure, however, all lived cosseted lives and were born into wealth. However that may be, people who have accepted personal responsibility for their well-being and continue to do so as they age can prevent much in the way of ill health and accidents. Those who do not are often beset with problems in their later years. When they fall, they became frightened and more careful, which gives them an unnatural gait and makes them hesitate as they walk.

I could feel for my students, for I also endured a period when I couldn't walk without crutches. The compound spiral fracture I sustained when I broke my tibia and fibula should have healed in three or four months. But it took a year. At the outset, I had a pin through my heel that butted out like a kebab. The pain was unbearable, and I could sleep only on my back. Moving meant having my caregivers wheel me around like a helpless child. I could use crutches, but only if they were in reach. I developed a terrible fear of falling. Because the body remembers fear, panic or anxiety can result. And fear, panic and anxiety are difficult to reprogram, particularly as we age. My tough, hardy exterior and the commitment that I could cope with any disaster – one I had worked so hard to develop – all but deserted me. I still can't explain the extent to which constant, unrelenting pain depleted my resources, mental, emotional, and physical. But I also knew I would recover, whereas my students lived in the likely knowledge that they would never improve. With all my philosophizing, I came to realize that, in their condition, I might not have done nearly as well. But the accident did help me better understand what the elderly around me were enduring; I came out of it much more sympathetic and better prepared to undertake my work and improve my students' lives.

Chapter Eleven

Where did the Bluebirds over the White Cliffs of Dover Go?

No man is an island entire to himself, everyman is a piece of the Continent part of the main. Any man's death diminishes me ... therefore, never send for whom the bell tolls, it tolls for thee.
—John Donne

The rampant depression in the homes I visited didn't surprise me. I myself had experienced serious postnatal and recurrent winter depression, so severe that I was once hospitalized with a nervous breakdown. I understand now that the depression emanated from a lack of coping skills and an abundance of fear. People enduring recurrent depression ostensibly fall into two categories: the martyrs, who play tough and don't want any help; and those who rely on others for help rather than looking inward. The road to salvation, however, lies between these extremes.

Two turning points helped me overcome and finally defeat recurring deep depression. The first was when I learned that depression is anger turned inward and that it emerged when I felt out of control, powerless to effect change in my life. The second followed on my family doctor referring me to an elderly psychiatrist. The psychiatrist's office was on Wimpole Street, a part of the city replete with renowned doctors. He was a quiet, kindly grandfather type. Within five minutes, he diagnosed me with a sexual problem. He laid me on a couch where he hypnotized me and had me open my blouse and bra. He hypnotized me again on my second visit. This time, he had me naked, with his middle finger going in and out of my vagina for what seemed like forever. He asked if I enjoyed the experience. As I stood up and dressed, he stayed very close, as if expecting an embrace. I left feeling quite disturbed, and I soon told my friends what had happened. But no one was prepared to stand up to him, and most people advised me to refrain from doing so. Still, the "treatment" was a turning point for me. I realized that if I allowed myself to sink so low, any pervert could take advantage of me. I believed I must have been crazy. The realization forced me to stop feeling sorry for myself. So, I got on with life, something I had always feared.

Insecure, frigid people who are prone to anxiety have the most difficult time coping with old age, when they become susceptible to depression as well. These individuals respond to stress negatively, rather than seeing it as a challenge and rising above it. Most likely, their life experiences have not armed them with appropriate responses. Instead, they react to stress and bad experiences by compensating and teaching themselves unacceptable ways to overcome problems, often with inappropriate behavior. Many men resort to passive aggressiveness. They cut themselves off to protect themselves from further pain or to assume the upper hand. Many pre-empt honest reaction by confronting every situation aggressively, mistakenly believing that this behavior gives them control.

As the arteries to the brain harden, constricting blood vessels by allowing less oxygenated blood to pass to cells, senile dementia occurs. This condition differs from Alzheimer's, although it is sometimes difficult to distinguish the two. I often wondered whether dementia was a protective escape mechanism that blocked out people's fears: after all, many of the senile people I met were obviously very fearful souls.

I believe there are two basic emotions, love and fear. Fear is an elastic word that encompasses negativity, including anger, envy, greed, jealousy, and desire. I didn't have to know what anyone was suffering from or why they were suffering: as I saw it, their condition always amounted to a form of fear and anger brought on by the absence of love. Negativity acts like a magnet that brings you face-to-face with that which you fear most. Women afraid of losing their looks may pile on more and more makeup – though beauticians will tell you that as you age, less is more. Those who fight too tightly to hold on to their youth often fail. The upshot is that they can't make the most of the next stage of their lives. "There's a time to plant and a time to sow." You can never force anything in life. By wanting something too much, you may be pushing it further away. Allow what is meant to be, and you are far more likely to achieve what you really need. Think about the people in their nineties who talk about their parents in the present tense – in the process becoming little children looking for security again.

What did surprise me, however, was how rarely the elderly mentioned their spouses. One exception, however, was a woman who insisted that she had to go home and make tea for her sons as their father was coming home from the army after years of fighting. That same woman, who usually looked so normal, suddenly erupted one day as my exercise class was underway, ranting and raving that this was her husband's funeral, and demanding that I stop the class immediately. She accused me of lacking respect for the dead and headed off to the main office where she insisted that they put a stop to the class.

The smallest nursing home I worked in consisted of two semi-detached houses knocked together. Three Alzheimer's patients walked incessantly from one end of the structure to the other, moving at a lively pace and pushing away anyone who crossed their path. Nor were they deterred when I erected chairs and frames to block their passage through my class. This being said, the to and fro did at times make the little home seem as busy as Piccadilly Circus.

As it turns out, many Alzheimer's patients have an urge to wander. More than a few times, and even in the dead of winter, I rescued individuals who had somehow escaped from the locked homes and were roaming the streets randomly. Perhaps they were acting on the primitive instinct that compelled them to return somewhere to die. Zsa Zsa, 60 years old, lived in an upmarket, suburban nursing home where the residents dressed meticulously. She never ventured from her room without earrings and a full complement of jewelry. One day, she wandered off to the Strand, some eight miles away. Fortunately, an alert passerby rescued her.

Sara, a new resident a bit older than Zsa Zsa, suffered with Alzheimer's. They were remarkably alike and became inseparable companions. Sara became convinced that Zsa Zsa was her daughter who died while still a child. The upshot was that Zsa Zsa became so childlike that she could not form sentences, able only to utter baby-like gurgling noises. Eventually, staff moved the two women to a newly created Alzheimer's wing with locked doors. There they remained with others who were in a similar condition, having also moved on to the Twilight Zone.

Alzheimer's has many manifestations. At another home, a newly arrived Alzheimer's patient turned out to be aggressive, violent, and unaware or not caring that she was in public, swearing continuously and scratching herself in inappropriate places. She didn't last long before she was transferred elsewhere. Soon, staff started to recognize certain patterns, and having learned their lesson, quickly transferred out new residents who didn't fit the mold.

Edie, however, was an exception. A sweet old lady until she became increasingly violent, she remained in the home despite her deterioration. She had been there for a long time, and I guessed they just couldn't get rid of her. Over time, caregivers used to bait her and play games at her expense. Residents, expecting her outbursts, became pre-emptively aggressive toward her. For my part, I tried loving kindness as a way of breaking through to her. At first, she met my greetings and compliments with insults, complaining how terrible the music and the exercises were. Still, I approached her frequently, albeit within spitting but not striking distance. I continued to treat her respectfully, and eventually she began to participate in my class. I made it a point to tell her how well she moved. We shook hands and said goodbye as normal people might. Once again, respect had enhanced self-esteem, overcoming the reduced serotonin level that so often makes the elderly cranky.

What was remarkable was that feelings endure even as the disease progresses. The spirit, it seems, is always aware. Whenever the home played a popular song from the war years, for example, a window opened even for those in fairly advanced stages of Alzheimer's. They all remembered the tunes and lyrics to "Underneath the Arches," "The White Cliffs of Dover" and other significant melodies. Even Dorit, who otherwise seemed permanently engaged with her sweater, twisting and turning a corner every which way over and over and over, stopped and sang along. Still, many of the residents seemed as if all the vestiges of life had left them. Vegetables in the ground had more vitality. I tried to be attentive, and they all responded, but in their own way.

A new resident, Sonia, was screaming and shouting at the back of the large dining room/lounge. She was falling out of her chair, but no one bothered to notice, as if she was no more than background noise, like a construction drill outside one's window. I led her from her place in the farthest part of the lounge and sat her next to me. When she became disruptive, I preempted the behavior by putting my hand on her whenever I could. Touching, I always felt, made a special connection. The skin is full of receptors whose stimulation creates calm and a sense of security. Few residents resented or resisted the touch of another human being, and only one became aggressive in response. For her part, Sonia responded with kisses and thanked me for treating her so kindly – in an educated, refined voice that replaced the wolf-like howl that had preceded it. What had life done to her to drive her to such despair? Another resident, who looked like a gentle schoolmaster, spent all his time in low conversation with himself even as he rummaged through any handbag, jacket pocket or cupboard he could find – and kept doing so until someone led him back to his seat. But it wasn't long before he was up again, this time examining a book inside and out without really taking in any of it. His mind had obviously left what was still a healthy, strong body.

Leila, for her part, was unique, like no one I had ever encountered. Warm-hearted and endearing, she accompanied her entrances with noisy laughter that persisted until she settled. Long hair curling from her chin complemented short, straggly and unkempt gray hair. Her always-bare legs were swollen with unsightly skin, her feet in pink slippers with the tongues hanging out. Her hunched shoulders and arms, wound around her handbag, gave the impression that she was guarding Fort Knox. Once she appeared with a cup surrounded by tissues pushed into her blouse. That, she explained, ensured that no one touched and contaminated it. Her fear was phobic: she became angry whenever anyone in the room dared to sneeze. In fact, staff told me that Leila could be very difficult. She refused to sit on the toilet seat, leaving the surrounding floor soaked with urine. It was hard to believe, such a pleasure was she to be around, and so intelligent. But Leila was also a loner with many enemies in the home. She still had a keen interest in men, couldn't keep her eyes off any nice-looking males and flirted with them like a young girl. I imagine that she suffered from obsessive-compulsive disorder (OCD).

Another resident, Anastasia, of German origin, was an intelligent, mobile woman in her nineties who was nonetheless in a great deal of trouble. A depressive who didn't mix with others, she finally made up her mind that she had had enough of life. Staff found her on the floor of her room: she had slashed her wrists with broken glass. She returned from hospital in a sorry state, and not many weeks went by before she got her wish and passed away. Roslyn, who lived in a retirement home in leafy Hampstead, was yet another woman who chose to keep to herself, passing the time engrossed in her reading. But she did it because she felt intellectually superior and better educated than her peers, who were mostly tradespeople. They included Joe, a fruiter seller who rose at 4 a.m. all his working life to buy fresh produce at market. Having spent a lifetime serving customers from the display outside his shop in all kinds of weather, he wore only a sweater even when temperatures were coldest. Debbie, officially blind but able to see a bit from time to time, had worked behind the counter in a pub. Others had been seamstresses, dressmakers, hat makers, and taxi drivers.

Roslyn had been a bookkeeper in a law firm. She had the appearance of a bag lady, always carrying around parcels wrapped in plastic bags. An unpleasant odor also accompanied her, leading others to abuse her until she settled down. Even then, no one would sit anywhere near her. Roslyn had many altercations with the head of home and complained so bitterly that she was finally transferred elsewhere. Unfortunately, the new home was far worse than the old one, largely because the residents were severely mentally and physically handicapped. She found herself in an enormous room filled with screeching people, in an environment that had more in common with a zoo than a nursing home.

Alfred had lost his marbles. His clothing was always all over the place. He would spit up phlegm frequently, revolting everyone around him, including myself, and regularly staining his apparel. Like Roslyn, the residents regularly abused him. Sadly, the truth was that collective bullying was commonplace and residents never welcomed newcomers.

Elsie arrived at a nursing home after experiencing a stroke and spending two years in the bedroom on the first floor of her house. She had had little physiotherapy and had done nothing toward regaining movement in her left side. Covered with a blanket from shoulders to toes, she presented as a complete invalid. Still, I encouraged her to take part in the class, doing what she could with the side of her body unaffected by the stroke. When she finally sat up, at my direction, she discovered that her lame arm could move much more than she had bothered to realize. Soon, she started moving her shoulders and other dormant muscles. She took part enthusiastically in the next class as well and continued to progress. So I was taken aback the following week when the head of home told me that Elsie's family had complained that she was unhappy about the exercises: they no longer wanted her to participate. I understood exactly what happened and so did the head. Despair had become a way of life for Elsie. Her brain was constantly firing off negativity. She couldn't cope with the sudden rush of happy sensations and good feelings she experienced through the music and movement. It opened up too many emotional doorways to her wasted years. When I next encountered her, back in her usual position, she returned my greeting with a sardonic expression.

Rita was losing her memory, so her children forced her into a home. She was a lovely woman, however, and made friends easily. But the home was locked and her freedom to leave the premises restricted. Rita couldn't cope, falling into misery and distress. She wanted to be home where she was prepared to cope with the loneliness and lack of assistance. She valued her freedom, fought for it, and eventually went back, returning occasionally as a visitor. Looking back, I see now that Rita exemplified our society's tendency to force individuals with diminished mental and physical capacities into care prematurely. The reality is that that we all know what we need, albeit our needs may be buried in our subconscious: others should respect that.

My mother-in-law, Isabelle, lived in sheltered housing in a small flat attached to a nursing home. She had a view of the sea and was happy there. She prepared her own breakfast when she awoke, usually at 4 a.m., returning to bed thereafter and rising again at 8. She joined the other residents for lunch but cooked her own evening meal, for which she did the shopping. She also entertained her family, preparing food for them from time to time. Unfortunately, she left the water on in the kitchen on a few occasions, flooding the flat below. After the fourth incident, the head of home insisted that my mother-in-law move to the nursing facility when a room became available. She also maintained that Isabelle was a danger to herself and others when she crossed the road. She thought it significant that Isabelle could not write a cheque. Her age, the head concluded, demanded that she give up her independence. Isabelle, however, couldn't and wouldn't accept losing her freedom and privileges. She kicked up an enormous fuss and won the battle. Management adapted by installing taps that turned the water off automatically. By way of celebration and at age 93, she flew off to South Africa with us for a two-week holiday – during which I sometimes had trouble keeping up with her. Eventually, however, Isabelle became a bit confused. She accepted a move into the nursing area. Shortly afterwards, she developed a paranoid feeling that a woman was stealing from her. The home put a lock on Isabelle's door, and she wore the key around her neck constantly. But the accusations persisted. The truth was that the accused woman was an old friend whom Isabelle felt had betrayed her. Accusing the woman of theft was Isabelle's way of dealing with the hurt. It would have been far better for her to make another friend, but she couldn't do so. Eventually, doctors prescribed drugs to help her anxiety.

Maud, in her mid-nineties, never missed a class. Locked in darkness and silence, she was nonetheless intelligent, refined and genteel. She could barely see or hear and walked slowly and laboriously, one leg shorter than the other. So bad was her hearing that I had to scream exercise instructions in her ear and direct her movements through touch. I once asked how she managed to remain so cheerful. She seemed embarrassed by my question. Her reply was that she was grateful to be so well looked after. She was one of the rare individuals I encountered who embodied the principles that I valued and hope still to master. But the ones who did were full of love in their hearts and never complained of their pain and suffering. They still had a place for the welfare of others, even for those who were not nearly as debilitated as they were. These are the people who were my heroes.

Maud was one of them. The cozy residential home in which she lived, part of a charitable trust, was one of my favorites. Both the head of home and her deputy were straightforward and kind. The home was a simple place where Maud didn't get special attention. Apart from meals, she spent most of her time on her own – except for the intrusions of Gertrude, who had made Maud her personal business, always sitting beside and fussing over her. Oddly enough, Gertrude on her own was obnoxious and not at all likeable. But she was competent and sprightly. Eventually, after falling ill, Maud deteriorated. She lost interest in my classes and was no longer cheerful and easygoing. She slept longer and longer until, one day, she woke no more.

Soon after Maud died. Gertrude, confused, escaped from the home on a very cold day. I found her wandering down the road, without a coat. As time passed, she changed from the person I had known (and couldn't stand) to a docile and sweet personality. Seven years in, she started taking part in the exercise classes and enjoying life. She celebrated her 102nd birthday in good form, her faculties intact. By the next year, however, decline had set in and she could no longer walk unsupported, a condition I attributed less to physical disability than to fear and mental decline. However that might be, her transformation assured me that every life was worth the effort and time I expended.

Tessa was another genteel, well-spoken resident, who had lived in the same home for 12 years. She was painfully thin, her bones protruding from her clothes. The pain in her joints, gnarled with arthritis, must have been agonizing, but she was a brave, stoic woman who never complained, getting around with the aid of an elevated frame that moved on wheels. Only once, as she was moving through the door to the garden, which was surfaced differently, did I see her distressed. Afraid of falling, she panicked. But that was the only time she displayed outward emotion.

Tessa's only friend had passed on several years earlier. A spinster who had lost touch with her family, she didn't speak to anyone at the home but did participate in my class. I, and the senior caregiver, the daughter of her late friend in the home, were the only ones who attended her funeral. For my part, I considered it a blessing to follow a person to their grave. I was proud to be there.

Alice was another of those rare individuals who never complained about her distorted body. She preferred discomfort to asking for assistance yet was always so cheerful and concerned for others. She spent her days sitting in a chair, surrounded for the most part by demented and handicapped individuals. I wondered how Alice could maintain her goodness in her difficult circumstances. The caregivers, who appeared untrained, and nurses at her home were mostly rotating agency staff who had little regard for their charges. The residents had only some visits from family and a local priest to break up the monotony of their sad lives.

Ella was another of my heroes. She woke up one morning paralyzed from the waist down. After that, she spent mornings in bed and afternoons in the lounge with others. Fortunately, this nursing home was well-maintained and warmly decorated, which helped alleviate the residents' difficult circumstances. Still, Ella hated sitting in her uncomfortable and restraining wheelchair. Yet moving her to a chair was too much "trouble" for the ample staff standing around doing nothing. To Ella's credit, she did mix with other residents. Her only frequent visitor, however, was her beloved son. But she tried to spend her time productively. She loved the exercises and never missed a class. When the rest of the class did leg movements she couldn't manage, she improvised with her hands. Her determination was remarkable. Ella also looked after herself. She always wore lipstick and brushed her hair. Despite the fact that she had only a few simple dresses, her choice of the day was always an important one. The reason I knew so much about Ella's boudoir was that the staff forgot her when they were busy or short. But I made it my business to have staff bring her downstairs and assisted them in getting her ready. Though hopelessly dependent, requiring the aid of a pulley and two caregivers to raise herself, she always did the best she could, never demanding that anyone fuss over her.

With few exceptions, women outnumbered men tenfold. Most old men tended to grumpiness, and just three stand out for their kindly dispositions. Simon, for one, was of Viennese origin, a perfectionist with an uptight disposition softened by old world charm. He was obsessive about sitting in the same chair. Always properly turned out, he spent hours reading and took part in my classes, where he was forever casting dirty looks at anyone who saw fit to disturb the proceedings. It was very sad to see Simon lose his mind as he aged. He started forgetting where he was or where he had been. To make matters worse, becoming old incensed him. Then there was Stan, who despite a humble background, had made money in construction. He was the only person who ever insisted on giving me a tip, insisting that he couldn't take the ten pounds he offered "with him" and that it would give him pleasure if I accepted. I really appreciated the thought and his kindness. As it turned out, he was right about not "taking it with him": he died a few months later. The third man, Ben, seemed ancient, but he had a saintly disposition and never admitted he couldn't hear a word I said – which produced some strange conversations.

Out of the hundreds of people I met, the aforementioned men and women stood out for their loving kindness, selflessness, courage, humility and warm hearts. What became clear to me over the years was that mental attitude, not ailments, dictated the elderly's quality of life. Indeed, Victor Frankl, the eminent Viennese psychologist, believed it was attitude that created meaning in life. "It isn't what you bear, it's the how," Frankl said – and Edie was the supreme example.

Walking with a frame, she was 93 when she arrived at the small nursing home, presenting as the sweet little old fairy tale grandmother one envisages in a children's story. An elastic band pulled back her thin gray hair into a sort of bun, her body so slim that her skin was taut over her lined face. The top digits of the first fingers on both her hands were missing. Although Edie had not exercised previously, she attended and enjoyed my class and my music, and worked harder at the exercises than she should have. I always had to slow her down so she could catch her breath. Eventually, she fell ill. I watched her deteriorate. Not only could she no longer join the classes, but she also couldn't even move herself from her chair, Still, "hopefully next week," was her mantra. Next week, of course, never came. But to the end, she stayed strong, graceful, positive and hopeful.

These people had the power to change and improve, as we all do. Unfortunately, they didn't always have the required stimulation or motivation. They, like many of us, had untapped inner talents that went to naught for lack of opportunity or inspiration.

Chapter Twelve

Nazi Child Rearing

*For what shall it profit a man, if he shall gain the whole world and
lose his own soul?*
—St. Mark

Are our lives predestined, mapped out for us before we were
born? How much choice and free will do we really have? Did
Adam and Eve, alone in the Garden of Eden with two fruit trees,
really have free will and choice? Wasn't it inevitable that Eve
would pick a fig from the Tree of Knowledge?

Benjamin Libet, an American physiologist, showed in the
eighties that the brain knows what decision a person will take
before the person becomes aware of it. His conclusion was that
"There is no such thing as Free Will." The truth is, however,
that the decisions we take result from both nature and nurture,
our genes and our environment. Chemicals in our brain control
our perceptions, meaning our neurophysiology is responsible
for our actions. But how can we be entirely responsible for our
conduct and choices when we don't choose our parents, our
environment, and our individual physiology? In the end, we
choose either what gives us pleasure or what gives us pain.

In 1934, Johanna Haarer authored child rearing books aimed
at developing hardened followers and soldiers who would
serve Hitler and promote Nazi goals. Mothers were taught to
ignore their babies' emotional needs, thereby depriving the
children of attachment and affection, in the belief that they
would grow up to be tough, unemotional, unempathetic, and
form only weak bonds with others. Millions of households had
a copy of Haarer's *German Mother and Her First Child*. By April
1943, at least three million German women had experienced an

indoctrination program based on Haarer's ideas. Pictures in Haarer's books showed mothers holding their children in ways that ensured they had as little contact as possible. Children, especially babies, were viewed as nuisances, whose wills needed to be broken. "The child is to be fed, bathed and dried off, and apart from that left completely alone," Haarer wrote. She recommended that parents isolate their children for 24 hours after birth; and that the mother should speak to her child only in sensible German and "If the child cries, let him cry." As for sleep time:

> It is best if the child is in his own room where he can be left alone. If the child starts to cry it is best to ignore him. Whatever you do, do not pick the child up from his bed, carry him around, cradle him, stroke him, hold him on your lap or even nurse, otherwise the child will quickly understand that all he needs to do is cry in order to attract sympathy and become the object of caring. Within a short time, he will demand this service as a right, leave you no peace until he is carried again, cradled or stroked and with that a tiny but implacable house tyrant is formed.

The work remained popular even after the war and enjoyed publication for decades. Indeed, Haarer's methods are still believed to contribute to Germany's low birth rate, high incidence of isolation, burnout, depression and emotional illness. A disproportionate number of Germans are disgusted at their own bodies, suffer eating disorders, and remain devoid of close relationships. Worse still, studies conducted in the 1970s showed that children raised in this way passed their attachment issues to the next generation.

There is a parallel, ironically, among Jews. Children of Holocaust survivors are now known as "second generation survivors," defined by their parents' demons, though knowing little of their history. After the war, many Holocaust survivors, anxious to rebuild their family lives, entered into loveless marriages that deprived them of the tools they needed to develop positive self-images. Survivor parents tended to be overprotective, some say to the point of suffocation. Their children existed to replace what was lost, rather than growing up in their own image. But although children can be traumatized across generations, parents can also pass on resilience and adaptability. So many of these children are tribal and task-oriented, with strong family values. Close bonds exist between grandparents and grandchildren. Cross-generational communication abounds, so that by the fourth generation, the wounds have healed.

Six weeks before my twentieth birthday, I left my parents and family in the US to marry an Englishman and live in England. Three years later, I flew back to comfort my brother in his last weeks. After his death, my greatest need was to grieve and mourn with my family. I refused to return to the UK or my marriage. My parents, unable to cope with my leaving the marriage, forced me back, claiming it was best for me. Back in London, I cried myself to sleep for four months. Then the crying stopped, but for many decades my eyes welled-up at the mention of my brother. It has been suggested to me that my relationship with Henry, into which I put so much effort, was not entirely altruistic and could have been a transference – a replay of my relationship with my brother, who was Henry's age when he died. Would my life have turned out differently had my parents allowed me to remain in the US with them long enough for time and their love to heal me? Whatever the answer to that question, it led me to my quest for meaning in life, which had ended so abruptly for my brother.

I divorced my first husband a few years later and remarried 20 years later. A photo soon emerged of my first mother-in-law, arm in arm with my second mother-in-law in Brighton in the 1930s. My first father-in-law had been the photographer. Even more strange was the similarity of experiences these young women were to share, albeit in disparate environments. Both women married, had second children that died, and conceived again to console their grief. My husbands' families were of similar backgrounds, both very different and somewhat alien to mine. I found it hard to fathom that I had married two men, one from London and the other from nearby Southport, whose parents had known each other and both of whom were conceived to replace a lost sibling. How bizarre. On the other hand, it all led me to believe that there is a plan for each and every life. We aren't meant to know the plan, leaving our will free to choose how we play out our hand.

Chapter Thirteen

How Much Is that Doggy in the Window?

It matters not how a man dies, but how he lives. The act of dying is not important, it lasts so short a time.
—Samuel Johnson

The extreme conditions of my students made my work varied and interesting. Still, I took everyone in the class as I found them and tended to forget that they were special with unique needs. It wasn't until I attended a Christmas party at a center for learning disabilities, where I sat in the audience as an outsider and not a teacher, that their uniqueness struck me fully.

Particularly memorable were two middle-aged men and a woman whom I didn't know and who didn't seem out of the ordinary – at least not until they began to sing "How much is that doggie in the window?", a performance which featured one of them barking along for the chorus.

The most seriously handicapped group I taught consisted of middle-aged people with multiple learning and physical disabilities. I didn't meet them often because their home was always short-staffed and couldn't get them out in time to arrive at my class. There was little I could do with them, as they couldn't really respond. One woman looked as if she might, but although she looked like she was present, she wasn't. Only one man in the group could speak and communicate. Unlike the others, he was able to feed himself, albeit with assistance. The group wasn't quite right for him: he likely fell between the cracks as a bit too helpless to reside in a facility for people with pure learning disabilities who could perform rudimentary tasks for themselves.

I only went to their home once. It was a large, modern,

purpose-built residence with a good-sized living-dining room and a nice, homey atmosphere. There were toys in one corner, as if it were a family home with young children, and a large TV in the other. The residents ate in a separate room off the kitchen. But they presented almost like babies. Sarah, a small, thin woman locked in a distorted body, could walk a bit with assistance from two caregivers. At one point, I got excited as I believed Sarah was really responding in class. But it turned out that the smile on her face was a reaction to gas or discomfort, and her movements were merely reflex actions. Marvin, large and strong, was nonetheless confined to a wheelchair and needed two muscular male caregivers to look after him. He could have been handsome, but for the childlike way his tongue wagged out of his mouth. He couldn't speak other than by grunting and grabbed anyone who came near him without letting go. Paula had dark curly hair that revealed gray strands. She could communicate only through smiles and tears. When she tired, she cried endlessly and couldn't be hushed, unable to settle unless in familiar surroundings with people she knew.

She would constantly look at her watch, then out the window, and then out the door.

Despite the students' limitations, the class was warm and friendly. Held in close proximity, it exuded a palpable energy. The music and movement delivered all to another stratosphere – remarkably so, as no one ever moved from their chair. It's still difficult to describe the elation I felt. The many moving experiences I had with this unfortunate group, whose opportunities for self-expression were so limited, confirmed for me that the receiving is indeed in the giving and that life is all about "loving the stranger."

Simone belonged to yet another group in this center for learning disabilities. One day she was the only student in attendance. So we had a private lesson. It took a long time to get her to tap her toe and heel in different sequences. She was impelled to interrupt and take brief rests, during which she went on about the burger and Coke she would be having at the Burger Shop. Apart from gardening, her chief occupation in warm weather, she couldn't seem to grasp much more than the concept of a burger. The experience reminded me of my young grandsons' reaction to their first vacation, in the south of France, where they enjoyed many special rides and amusements: all they could talk about was the ice cream.

Individuals with different degrees of learning difficulties populated my class, whom I separated accordingly. The Wednesday morning group was an interesting mix of people slow to grasp the basic techniques of movement, and who remained at more or less the same level throughout. For example, Rachel, who had spent two years attending my class and who liked popular music and dancing, nonetheless found it difficult to keep to the beat and co-ordinate her movements to the music. Now in her mid-twenties, she could not relate to others or make eye contact with them. Another group member, Alan, became upset when he thought I was displeased with him, something he professed each week. Sixtyish and slow of movement, he became bored quickly and lacked enthusiasm, leaving him present physically but elsewhere mentally. Steve, on the other hand, was very keen on and knowledgeable about classical music. He had an amazing memory for birthdays, dates and numbers, but couldn't function at work. Sylvia, in her late forties, had Down's Syndrome and was affectionate but shy, a mad football fan who liked clothes and nail polish. She had the benefit of a flexible, double-jointed body that is common to many afflicted with Down's. She often hung by the wall at a distance from others. On the infrequent occasions that I managed to draw her to the circle, she rarely did more than sit. On the odd occasion when she participated, I praised her for her flexibility and suppleness. I was very surprised when she told me she had slept with a male caregiver. I reported the incident but never heard back. Camilla was not unlike Sylvia.

She was also into the latest music, clothes and boys. I never saw either her or Sylvia conversing with any of the other students. She would, however, open up a bit at times and chat with me and other caregivers.

Flora was someone with whom I had a problem. Depressed and unhappy for the most part, her mood never infringed on her participation in the exercises. But she had a habit of conversing with others during the class, especially someone on the opposite side of the circle. When I asked her to be quiet, she became aggressive and blamed me for not being nice. She could never, it seemed, manage to be pleasant for very long. Flora did like Sophie, also in her late forties, who was always formally attired and adorned in bright jewelry and scarves. But Sophie couldn't sit still for long, and often left the room after a short while. In this way, she was like most of the rest of the class: unable to focus or concentrate for any length of time. Still, they all seemed to get something from their participation.

I also worked with a much younger teen-aged group. They were an endearing bunch despite their handicaps, and I saw them as the lovely souls they were. Some appeared to be on the extreme end of the autistic spectrum, and all needed individual attention. No one could get near Ann, for example, as she was inclined to pull people's hair very hard. My energy and enthusiasm hardly seemed to make a difference. Perhaps, at the very least, they found the music uplifting and the exercise advantageous. Studies, after all, have shown that exercise can bring marked improvement in autistic children. When all was said and done, however, I enjoyed some of the most uplifting moments of my life with these students. To help them, I had to dig deep inside myself. And the greater my effort, the greater was my reward. Even when I could not see that I was making an iota of difference to their lives, doing my best was my reward: "Nothing good comes without toil and according to the toil can be known the harvest."

Chapter Fourteen

Special Children

Focus your light like a laser into an intense powerful beam.
— R. Menachem Mendel Schneerson

Introducing me to a kaleidoscope of society was one of the primary ways in which my work enriched my life. There was always a new group with different needs. One that stands out included individuals whose ages ranged from their early twenties to their late fifties. They had a variety of psychiatric disorders, but all were deemed harmless, which was the sole criterion for their membership at this particular day center.

Among them was Eamon, a sweet boy in his mid-twenties who was afflicted with Asperger's, a form of autism that affected the way he related to and socialized with others. Like others with his condition, all was black and white to him. But these individuals are often very intelligent and persistent in their hobbies and interests. Routine is important to them, and they find change difficult. They can lack co-ordination and are generally clumsy. Eamon, who called himself Mark when not in my class, tried hard to overcome his handicap by focusing fiercely on his body, which included obsessive exercise. He enjoyed the class and did extremely well in it as it coincided with his need for control. But, like many things in his life, his attendance, restricted to Tuesdays, was a ritual. Indeed, he was so obsessive that he took down the curtains in his home every day and put them back up at night. And he always made sure the doors were closed to the room where the class took place. I taught Eamon how to control his body. He succeeded in isolating muscle groups and went on to lose quite a lot of excess weight. But he couldn't dance to fixed steps; every few minutes found him scratching his testicles and shouting out to others. Over time, he learned to control the chatter and progressed well.

Unfortunately, and suddenly, everything changed for Eamon. His home life became unsettled when his father brought in a new woman. As Eamon perceived it, women now posed a threat to his ordered and settled life. Females in general became the focus of his anger as he transferred his enmity for his father's partner to each and every member of the opposite sex, including participants in my class and staff. Surprisingly, perhaps, he did not include me in his wrath: it seemed that he perceived me as a teacher helping him achieve his goals, and my gender didn't enter into it. So intense was Eamon's fear or dislike of women that I found him hiding in curious places to avoid then. Many meetings and promises to change his behaviors went for naught, and in the end he was barred from the center, a heartbreaking end to another sad story.

Others had different stories. Morris, in his thirties, was obviously troubled. He wouldn't stop talking but made little sense. His sentences were garbled and his words aimless. Barbara, suffering from schizophrenia and depression, was a pretty little thing who had been unsuccessful in her attempts to live in the outside world. She didn't get along with her parents, and her sister also suffered from schizophrenic attacks. Nonetheless, she was a pleasant girl whose issues were not at all apparent in my class, where she did really well.

At times, however, Barbara wasn't her usual cheery self. On these occasions, her face was white, her eyes didn't have their usual brightness, and eventually her breathing became shallow. It turned out that she suffered with asthma and was undergoing hypnosis to overcome it. In class, I helped her control her breathing, which alleviated her condition. Sometimes, though, I wondered if the asthma was less physically induced than a state of mind. On another occasion, Barbara stopped participating. She said her mind was troubled. I told her that, as a child, I handled nightmares by going over the dream after I awoke and changing its course to a more pleasing resolution. I suggested that she try to change her thoughts by acknowledging that they were bad thoughts, then concentrate on the music and just follow the exercises. As everyone in the class relaxed their necks, tilting our heads to the side so our ears almost touched our shoulders, Barbara found that she was able to carry on, and she left relaxed and happy.

Gerry was another Asperger's sufferer, which inhibited his ability to empathize and react properly to social situations. For example, he tended to continue his conversations whether anyone was listening or not. Gerry saw my classes from an academic perspective – a way to improve his mind. He approached the exercises intellectually rather than athletically. And he always wore the same clothes, regardless of the season, suggesting he was not in touch with his environment. He also gave off an unpleasant odor at times. On the other hand, he did look smart, very Chelsea in a Barbour shirt, a checked sports jacket, a dark blue wool V-neck sweater, checked shirt, woolen tie, and corduroy trousers. Another group member, Estelle, a middle-aged spinster with a sweet nature and pretty smile, was withdrawn and depressed. But she threw herself into exercise classes four times a week and became very flexible. Although she had no staying power or concentration and tended to drift off, I kept her engaged by bringing her back as soon as I noticed her wander.

I tried to give my students a sense of control over their lives, but also make them realize not to fight it if they weren't in control: I explained that just going with it until it passed was itself a measure of control. I concentrated on their breathing to ground and center them. I tried to make them aware of their tension and how it blocked the flow of blood and energy. I explained how proper posture enhanced that flow, while poor body placement slowed it down. Feeling in control increased their self-esteem, improved their self-confidence and gave them a sense of empowerment, at least momentarily. A few of my students, however, didn't have the option of influencing, changing or controlling any part of their lives. They were given a life sentence at birth that perpetually kept them in a penitentiary without walls. Time was all they could do.

Many people have commented on how depressing my work must have been. To the contrary, it was a true joy and the most rewarding experience of my life. The more needy the person, the greater the challenge and the satisfaction I felt – so much so that my work gave my life even more meaning. The greatest rewards come from reaching into the well of love that permeates us all. In giving, however, individuals must first and foremost respect themselves and preserve their dignity.

Reincarnation is the cycle of birth, life, death and rebirth where life's purpose is to gain ultimate knowledge and free oneself from the constraints of the material world through good deeds. It makes sense of a world where children born with severe disabilities are on their last journey in the cycle. There is a reason and purpose for each of these lives who have little to accomplish or any obligations. It is the parents of these children who are blessed and given the opportunity of caring for a soul who will always be dependent on them. These elevated beings cannot express their eminence but whose parents are given the task of looking into their own souls and hearts, to obtain their greatest joy. The disabilities for which there are no cure, deem these children unable to reveal their true inner selves, because of their souls' greatness and perfection that ordinary people cannot communicate with them. It is those who understand the blessings, that come with those who are children for this life. For believers, there is another "world to come."

Chapter Fifteen

Putting Meaning into One's Life

We determine what the significance of our life is, something you create yourself.
— Noam Chomsky

How do we achieve enlightenment? We need to let go. And letting go means allowing our minds to become an empty slate by relinquishing preconceived ideas, paradigms and judgments. Letting go is a lengthy and difficult process. It requires permitting our "inner voice" and feelings to direct how we live our lives. Personal guidance can be of great assistance in this journey. But some individuals, dedicated to living life by its natural laws, have achieved enlightenment on their own.

Wendy Hughes was one such person. Born in 1948 in a small town in Wales, her mother was 46, an age when the possibility of conceiving a first child is very low. Her father passed away when Wendy was five, but she remembered him and their happy home: father, mother and daughter were a close unit and their home full of love. When Wendy turned 8 years old her mother totally lost her sight, something that many believed resulted from the trauma caused by her husband's death. Wendy ended up in foster homes and had a difficult upbringing. When she was old enough, she returned home to look after her mother. Life was never easy for Wendy. But she had a strong foundation of love and security that provided her with the coping skills to face the many challenges in her life, including a shortage of money and a congenital partially cleft palate that made speaking and eating difficult.

Wendy knew she was different from her peers but didn't know why. Her joints hurt and she couldn't run and play games with other children. She felt inferior, particularly in school, where she couldn't keep up and was too embarrassed to ask questions. To hide what she believed was her stupidity, she went to the library every day, trying to catch up. Because of her own poor eyesight, Wendy's mother hadn't noticed that her daughter couldn't see without holding objects close to her face. She had, however, observed that Wendy had difficulty hearing and was oblivious to certain sounds. Although her disabilities went undiagnosed until Wendy was almost 40, she got through school and found employment. She was also extremely fortunate to meet and marry a man who recognized and appreciated her strengths and virtues. The couple shared household chores, and Wendy's husband remained steadfast during her frequent bouts of ill health. They had two normal, healthy babies.

But despite her happy marriage, life for Wendy was always a personal battle. She was perpetually in and out of hospital as her overall condition deteriorated. Finally, when she was almost 40, she was rushed to hospital with bilateral retinal detachment. The rectifying operation was a failure, and one week after discharge, she was back in hospital. By a stroke of luck, she encountered a medical student who had that day been reading about a common but often undiagnosed condition. He referred her to Moorfields Eye Hospital for a second opinion. That was the turning point. Moorfields doctors discovered a genetic fault in her DNA that had resulted in the improper formation of her body's connective tissue. The condition is known as Stickler Syndrome, for which there is no treatment, but it meant that the mortar between the bricks of Wendy's body was substandard and crumbling. Now she understood why her speech was impaired, why she had trouble eating, why she was always in pain, and why she was different from others.

So, Wendy remained in constant pain, her body slowly disintegrating. But she knew who she was and her purpose in life. Her calling was to help others with this condition. She founded an international support group and became an expert on Stickler Syndrome, offering advice to afflicted families as well as treating professionals. She ran a helpline for sufferers, published 800 articles all over the world, and wrote the only book on the condition. Medical professionals bought half the print run. She also authored works about her native Wales and other subjects. What is truly remarkable is that she could hardly see when she walked into the library to research *Stickler, the Elusive Syndrome*. Many times, she felt some power was guiding her to the shelf that had the right book or article. Similarly, "chance" meetings helped further her goals, and despite her lack of training, she always found the right words to comfort the desperate and despairing who suffer from the disease. Wendy was 70 when she died, leaving behind a loving husband, two adoring sons, and many grateful admirers.

Wendy obviously fulfilled her purpose. Many others don't. A case in point was Rita, an attractive woman with enormous charm and personality. An only child, her parents doted on her. She married Philippe, a successful businessman. The couple had four children and lived in a lovely house on lush grounds in an exclusive neighborhood outside of Paris. But when Philippe became ill with increasingly difficult to live with, the idyll shattered. Eventually, Rita instigated divorce proceedings and threw Philippe out of their home, where she and the children continued living. After a few years, she married Fred, sharing with him the same bedroom she had shared with Philippe. Her children, distraught, never forgave her. Her relationship with them became increasingly strained, particularly with the youngest daughter, who had been close to her father until life became so difficult for him that he saw fit to end it.

When the children were able to fend for themselves, Fred and Rita moved to southern Italy. Rita's mother, whom Rita had tended since her father's passing, accompanied them. Fred died shortly after and Rita moved back to Paris, where her daughters lived. As they were not terribly welcoming, she departed alone for California, where she had to support herself, initially as a fashion designer and later as a perfume saleswoman in a luxury department store. But finances remained tight, forcing her to sell her jewelry to supplement her lifestyle.

Life became easier for Rita when she met a man with whom she eventually moved in. But the relationship was suspect: she never told him that she was five years older than he was. He even gave her a 65th birthday party without knowing that she had had one five years earlier. But he wouldn't marry her, and the couple parted after she gave him an ultimatum. Soon, she was back selling and spraying perfume, and never found another partner.

It wasn't long before Rita, at age 74, fell ill. Her youngest daughter, citing grievances, wouldn't allow Rita to recuperate at her home. The daughter conveniently forgot that her mother had flown across the world to support her when she lapsed into depression after discovering that her husband had been unfaithful. But Rita's youngest, her son, allowed her to stay in his Parisian apartment for a month while she recuperated; he stayed nearby, moving in with his girlfriend. Unfortunately, the recuperation didn't go well. Complications arose, and Rita died of a heart attack in her son's apartment, alone with the remains of a sandwich that had recently been delivered.

The Fifth Commandment, which has no conditions attached, states simply, "Honor thy father and mother, that thy days may be long upon the land which the Lord thy God giveth thee." The mandate extends to all children, whether their parents are good, bad or indifferent. To be sure, the lack of respect Rita's children showed her stemmed from her own lack of compassion at their father's death – but it was still in breach of the Commandment. Somewhere in their hearts, however, they may have brought even deeper suffering upon themselves.

Brigitte, with her French accent and style, took another path.

She was a lively, cheerful, eighty, who still received admiring glances from younger men with whom she continued to consort. Her demeanor was in stark contrast to her terrible childhood, which included sexual abuse by her father. Her mother, similarly, abused, declined into mental instability and could not protect her daughter. Feeling unwanted, Brigitte was more or less on her own from her early years on. Understandably, she married young to escape her unhappy home. The marriage, and three others that followed, didn't last, but produced one daughter. Not surprisingly, perhaps, all her husbands shared an uncanny resemblance to her father in subjecting her to patterns of abuse.

Nonetheless, Brigitte supported her father in his old age after his wife predeceased him. She never confronted him and was always respectful. This, despite the fact that her traumatic childhood remained with her, so much so that she always required medication to help her sleep. Although she didn't bury her past and was open to discussing it, peace eluded her. That may be because she never owned the anger she must have felt. Still, she rose above her suffering and built a successful life.

Helen, kind-hearted, sporty, happy and always smiling, was yet another example of a beautiful woman whose childhood was devoid of love and affection. Abandoned as a baby, she was raised in an orphanage in Liverpool, where life among the nuns was harsh and cruel. She had no sense of family, carried a great deal of anger, and, like Brigitte, married young to escape her circumstances. When the teenage marriage failed in short order, Helen went to work in a fur shop and eventually became a designer for a large fashion house. Her tall, slim stature and beautiful face also led her to modeling, where she met her second husband and enjoyed a happy marriage. When her first husband died, Helen took up with another kindly man. Now in her mid-eighties but looking much younger and still taking great pride in her appearance, she was yet another woman who would not allow her past to define her.

But it wasn't always the individuals with a difficult upbringing who fared badly as they aged. I was quite surprised to learn, for example, that Bob was 86 years old. Tall and with an athletic build, he could have passed for his early seventies. He was a retired doctor who had suffered a stroke three years earlier but maintained some strength in his affected left side. I was confident that he could walk if he tried. However, Bob made no such effort, preferring to sit around feeling sorry for himself in the nursing facility where he lived. He liked the attention of his youthful, doting wife and the treats she would bring him. She also brought in three bridge players to play with her husband, a former bridge champion, but the weekly sessions appeared to have little effect: he had given up on living.

One of the people from whom I gained a great deal of insight about the older generation was my neighbor, dear Henrietta. She was in her late eighties when I met her, and we remained close for the next 10 years until her passing. As is too often the case, Henrietta's downfall came after a hip replacement. She had broken her hip when she tripped over her slipper as she got up to change the television station. Unfortunately, she knew very well that her family were "too busy" to bother with her. Like Rita, Henrietta grew up spoiled and wanting for nothing. She also married a man who catered to her whims. And like Rita again, her narcissistic and self-indulgent nature got in the way of a good relationship with her only son, who moved to Spain with her family after Henrietta's husband died. That left one granddaughter as Henrietta's only remaining family in England. The two spoke frequently but although her grandmother invited her to dinner weekly, Henrietta's granddaughter rarely saw fit to visit.

What impressed me most about Henrietta was how much fun she was. She was always lively and quick-witted, as were her close circle of widowed, but comfortable and well-off friends with whom she played Kaluki and Gin Rummy at least three times a week. All well-groomed, impeccably dressed and bejeweled, they shared the same hairdresser and manicurist, who attended them in their flats. They were all penny pinchers and reveled in a good argument. No surprise, then, that it was Henrietta – who ironically, perhaps, looked her age – who taught me that "Age is only a number."

Henrietta had another friend, Francesca, who lived in a secure block overlooking Hyde Park. But she didn't like being alone – perhaps because a governess had raised her in a sheltered environment and her parents had not permitted her to attend school – so she visited twice weekly in the afternoons, often staying until 10 p.m. Anxious not to be a bother, however, she always brought her own food. Francesca's sense of humor, her miserliness, and her capacity to swear like a trooper, surpassed even Henrietta's capacities. When Henrietta received a string of dirty telephone calls, Francesca grabbed the phone, giving back as dirty as she got. Some years older than Henrietta, she drove her car until she was well into her nineties and delighted in telling stories about her responses to younger drivers who might comment on her age. When Francesca finally gave up driving, she used free council transport to get around. Speaking in her plummy accent and cloaked in expensive clothes, her fellow passengers likely considered her a sight.

Henrietta maintained that she would never go to a nursing or retirement home. In fact, her entire circle died at home – one was even found dead on the floor. Henrietta's older sister, however, was whisked into a nursing home by her children when doctors diagnosed her with early onset Alzheimer's. At that point, she suffered from memory loss but didn't lack awareness. From an outsider's perspective, taking her from her home seemed a heartless act perpetrated by a son and daughter who couldn't otherwise be bothered. I took Henrietta to visit her sister, who spent her day in a small lounge on the top floor populated with advanced Alzheimer's patients. Here sat this once proud, handsome, elegant woman doing nothing but looking back at the blank faces around her. It didn't take long for her to deteriorate to their level: the next time I visited, she couldn't remember her sister's name or recognize her. What made all this so sad was that no one had tried to delay her deterioration. Henrietta, quite distraught after our visit, only saw her once afterward. Friends in the sister's inner circle didn't bother either: perhaps it was just too heartbreaking for them all. At one point, I had suggested that Henrietta get a housekeeper and take her sister in. But she, like her niece and nephew, wasn't inclined to inconvenience herself in her small apartment just to prolong her sister's quality of life. In some ways, that wasn't surprising. Henrietta's younger sister lived comfortably in a grand mansion flat nearby. I often asked Henrietta whether she wouldn't be better off if they lived together, but she loved her comforts and was not the sharing kind.

Perhaps it ran in the family: Henrietta's granddaughter, who resided nearby, never visited, although she and her husband did provide whatever Henrietta needed. But when Henrietta caught the flu, the granddaughter made it clear that she expected me to provide for her. With a full life of my own, I refused the exploitation, knowing full well that the family would only take my help for granted. So the family hired an *au pair* for emergencies. Henrietta enjoyed the company of the lively, young woman until a full-time Filipino caregiver replaced her.

Soon afterward, Henrietta started complaining about the caregiver. During one of my visits, Henrietta openly maligned the woman. The caregiver's retort was to tell her employer how her family hated her and didn't care about her. At the time, I said nothing, but gave the situation a lot of thought. The family was away, but I knew that I couldn't take Henrietta in. I contacted the nanny who ran the household and told her what I had witnessed. She was non-committal. When the granddaughter came back from holiday, she didn't return my call. The caregiver stayed on, treated like a queen by the family – who, incidentally, never acknowledged me or the important part I played in Henrietta's life. Eventually, I became *persona non grata*. Going forward, the only real time I spent with Henrietta was on the caregiver's (whom I named "Dragon") off day. Her replacement was also horrified at Henrietta's treatment, but, like me, she was powerless.

So, Henrietta continued to endure non-stop verbal abuse. For her part, the granddaughter visited only when the doctor came calling. But she wasn't satisfied with the excellent national health care physician who had looked after Henrietta so well for so long. He didn't want to do anything but leave her in peace. Instead, the granddaughter's younger and extremely expensive private doctor who replaced him changed her medications and subjected her to a myriad of tests. And the Dragon, always dressed in black, grew ever more powerful and arbitrary, even barring me when I came to the door with my daughter, whom Henrietta adored. There was no longer any doubt: Henrietta was the Dragon's prisoner. A few days later, she took sick and died quickly at the hospital.

But lives do end in many different ways. The very elegant memorial service in Farm Street church for Jean-Marc was packed with society figures and people drawn from the pages of *Tatler* and the social gossip columns in the tabloids. Jean-Marc was at every event on the social calendar. He had an early marriage, for money, which ended in tears for both, but did leave him with improved means. He had many friends, out lunching and dining daily. Hostesses sought him out as the "extra man." He was charming, vivacious, full of great stories and literally "sang for his supper." At the funeral, friends eulogized him, noting his numerous friends and how many parties he had attended. That was his life, and he lived it to the end.

I had the great fortune to befriend Charlie Sweeney during the last five years of his life. He was quite a character, who talked endlessly about business and the stock market, of which I knew nothing. But he did inspire me to take financial training courses that led to my passing the securities industries examinations. Charlie had lived a very full life, having been born with a silver spoon in his mouth. He was elegant, good looking, intelligent, a golfer and had broken many hearts. He frequented Scott's or Claridge's for lunch and Aspinall's for dinner after the Clermont Club closed down. During the war he founded the "Eagle Squadron," a group of American pilots who flew for Britain before the US entered the fray; a grand memorial in Grosvenor Square commemorates his achievement. Charlie maintained a good relationship with his son and daughter and was always there for his first wife, Margaret, who eventually became the Duchess of Argyll, a woman of some fame about whom books have been written.

Renowned for her beauty, charm, elegance and fortune, Margaret was the original "It" girl and on her fourth engagement, this time to the Earl of Warwick, when Charlie met her. Despite being untitled and American, he captured her heart, and their wedding befitted royalty. Although Charlie always worked, it was the support they received from their respective parents that enabled the grand lifestyle the young couple enjoyed. Charlie and Margaret had two children: a son, and a daughter who married a Duke. Charlie had many wonderful qualities, but he was not the ideal husband. They divorced 12 years into their marriage.

Margaret liked to travel and socialize, eventually marrying the Duke of Argyll, using her enormous zeal and munificence to salvage his crumbling estate and the Scottish town that housed it. But, as has been well documented, the marriage turned out to be an unsalvageable sham. And despite Margaret's attempts to sustain the relationship, it ended in a scandalous divorce in which the Duke spared no lengths to trample Margaret's reputation – already sullied by her penchant for litigation and previous salacious headlines. Despite all the dramas, Charlie remained loyal to her. Eventually, her fortune disappeared. Toward the end of her life, she moved into a room without private bath in a nursing home in Battersea in south London, where she ended her days sitting by the entrance, watching life elude her.

The life of Aristotle Onassis, once the richest man in the world, ended unenviably. He spent the last five years in conjugal horror with his ultimate trophy wife, Jacqueline Kennedy, whom he detested. Only the cost of a divorce and the secrets she knew kept him from divorcing her. Onassis was also paranoid, convinced his only son's helicopter "accident" was a score settled by his enemies. Perhaps he had reason for his fears: his first wife married his worst enemy, while his daughter attempted suicide and died not many years later. He was surrounded by sycophants who, primarily for their own sakes, protected his fortune and reputation from the treachery and criminality on which his empire was founded on. He was a man, however, who fully expected that his day of reckoning would not be rewarding.

Did these people have any control over their destinies? Could they have changed their fate? Despite being born into a life of poverty, hardship, and abuse, Wendy, Brigitte and Helen were shining examples of humanity's ability to rise from the ashes. They never blamed, complained or bemoaned their fates. They reconstructed their foundations and imagined a different future than the one fate seemed to have bestowed. By contrast, Rita, Henrietta and Margaret enjoyed lives of relative comfort and luxury. All had at least one parent who doted on them and they were raised to expect entitlement. But they were all self-centered and never formed close attachments with their children. Each died alone and practically destitute.

Chapter Sixteen

Spirituality

As for man — his days are like grass; like a flower of the field, for a wind passes over him and he is no longer here; and his place no longer recognizes him.
—Psalm 103, V15–16

Imagine the body as a car and spirit as its engine and driving force. When traveling on the wrong road, the journey is bumpy, a hissing sound comes from within, and the car sputters. On the right road, the vehicle sails along peacefully, feeling pure joy as it absorbs the beauty of nature.

Spirituality is about being part of the eternal. So is reincarnation, founded on the belief we live on in various guises after we die. The purpose of each rebirth is to give our spirit an opportunity to experience life again and correct past mistakes on the way to enlightenment. Adherents believe we are born with a purpose and choose our family, the body we inhabit, and the lessons we are to learn. The upshot is that families aren't haphazard, that children choose their parents, and that parents want to be the progenitors of these children. So it is with our friends, lovers, colleagues and other family members. Nothing is chance or coincidence: all is a result of the karmic seed blooming into season and erupting. Karma is the sum of our actions in successive states of existence. It is what determines our fate in the next stage. When karma from a previous life remains in the new life, we bear a heavier burden in reliving the previous life in the current one.

While swimming in the sea on a holiday in Costa Rica, I encountered a rip tide. I couldn't escape the current, nor did anyone hear my cries for help. Exhausted, I decided that the best course was to float and pray. But the waves kept taking me under. Suddenly, I saw people running along the beach to find me, led by my daughter, dressed in black. The experience convinced me of the existence of a parallel universe in which the people who were running along the beach had sighted my body. In my own universe, however, I had all but given up hope when I hit a sandbank and managed to get back to land, vomiting from fear all the way.

Spirituality is almost always part of religion but is not necessarily connected with God or a religion in itself. Rather, it is a belief in a higher power, energy, or force. It can be Jehovah, the Holy Spirit, Allah, Christ, Atman, Brahma, Buddha, Divine, Infinite Source, Krishna, Tao, the Force or manifest in many other ways. When used as intended, spirituality can help overcome the limitations of the physical world. Because its existence does not require conscious awareness, it allows a degree of control by attracting to ourselves the conditions of our lives. So, by way of example, behaving badly attracts not punishment but the conditions required to learn from mistakes. Spirit, then, is the traveling energy of the soul. Meditation enables the Spirit to leave the body and return to its Spirit group for revitalization, away from the toxicity of life on earth. Within each of us, then, lies the source of our enlightenment, wisdom and strength. We need only surrender to our spirits to obtain the necessary guidance. But it is a great surrender, greater than anything else, but also one that knows where we are going and what we need to get there.

When we feel something instinctively, it is the spirit that is driving us. We become aware of it through our feelings, which allow us to achieve a partnership that leaves us safe, that lets us search our soul for answers without expectation, that allows life to flow freely in the knowledge that there is an energy in charge of our life that will lead us to where we need to be. Just as dogs can hear at higher frequencies than people, there are individuals who can hear, feel and see things outside our normal sensory range. We refer to them as clairvoyants or clairaudients.

But everyone has psychic abilities, though we may call it heightened awareness or a sixth sense that enables us to pick up vibrations from others and make sense of them on a feeling level. At 2 a.m. one night, I woke with a start, certain something had happened to my mother. For 20 minutes, I agonized. But I didn't call her, thinking my feelings might just be the result of a bad dream and that she would be upset if I woke her. Suddenly, the phone rang. It was my mother, in terrible pain. She was having a heart attack. As we all know, such incredible, paranormal "coincidences" are not uncommon, and must surely be more than serendipity. We have recorded them from the beginning of time. And they take various forms, ranging from premonitions like mine to life-like dreams of the departed.

I know that my dreams have at times redirected me. To be sure, that doesn't amount to scientific evidence that paranormal activity exists – but its existence has never been disproved. I believe, however, that becoming aware of our sixth sense exposes us to vibration, past and present. Some people walk into a house and it evokes a feeling; a vibrancy permeates the air for some of us who have gazed at the wonders of Machu Picchu in Peru, where a well-preserved sixteenth-century Inca settlement stands atop a majestic mountain; at the Wailing Wall in Israel, an overwhelming feeling of power pervades; the Alexandra Palace in St. Petersburg, from whence Tsar Nicholas and his family were dispatched to Siberia, evokes a sense of gloom that infuses the magnificent surroundings. By contrast, visitors to Auschwitz and Birkenau concentration camps are sometimes amazed that they feel nothing. Some observers say that's because the camps' inmates were closely connected to their spirit group, albeit perhaps unaware of the connection. The Spirits, it is said, walked closely with the suffering and took them quickly when they died, drawing away and cleansing the camps of life and energy, leaving them desolate forever.

The Spirit, however, only takes shape or form when we surrender to it. This calls for a conscious acknowledgment of the supremacy of our spiritual identity over the limitations of our earthly vehicle, the body. Its release is dependent on recognition of all one can become. Everything depends upon believing that we are divine, that a part of us will not die. There are no boundaries as we move into our spiritual higher self, which makes itself known through our feelings and the suppression of our egos. The more we listen to it, the more powerful its ability to influence behavior by heightening intuition and awareness. The higher self, then, makes itself known through feelings. There is nothing, then, that one cannot strive for, do or succeed at. Indeed, the possibility of emancipating our Spirit means precisely that we are meant to strive, do, and succeed. Invariably, a path taken leads to unexpected and unforeseen opportunities. This is what is meant by the saying, "It's what the experience brings forth that matters, rather than the experience itself." If a door closes, accept it, reconsider, and live your life positively, knowing your Spirit is moving you forward.

The essence of all Divine relationships is the fulfillment of the law of love. Circumstances are irrelevant when we are in touch with the brightness of the inner light. True love entails accepting life as it is and drawing the power to improve our lives through the guiding force within. It is not what we do, it is the love with which we do it. It's the same love that accepts each of us as we are. This means we don't have to ask for love, it's there. We are composed of, born, and designed in love. It is not something we feel, but something we are. It is not something to possess, but something to give – and the more of it we give, the more of it flows back to us. It follows that wanting people to love us won't bring us love. Rather, love comes from turning on the fountain of love within: allow it to flow unconditionally and it self-perpetuates.

What are we really looking for in life? Those who seek happiness won't find it. Material or earthly goods are not the standard bearers for happiness. Avoid wanting and be happy with what you have.

Chapter Seventeen

The Greatest Love of All

I was 15 when they slaughtered my parents. I was taken to Auschwitz. I survived three years making uniforms. I was tortured, I was starved, I was frozen, I was beaten, but I survived as a tailor. The Red Army liberated us. I went to my Shtetl where there was no one else from my family left. Someone told me all the Jewish refugees have gone to Lodz. He gave me a few zlotys. When I got there I found someone from my state but no family. He was eighteen and I was fifteen. Like me he had lost everyone too. We applied to go to Israel and went from one displaced persons' camp to another and finally arrived in Israel. We married and I became pregnant. When we arrived, the Independence was starting, and my husband went to war. He never came back. My son was born, and I named him after my father, my father-in-law and my husband. I worked hard to pay for my son's education to give him a good life. I also bought him a home. If you visit my apartment, it's a museum. On one wall is a picture that someone gave me of my parents. I also had a picture of my husband and the rest of the wall is all covered with pictures of my son. My son is now twenty-five years old. The army came to synagogue when we were praying on Yom Kippur and all the young men who they called had to leave in preparation for the upcoming War. If he doesn't come back I have no reason to live. (Chief Rabbi Israel Meir Lau, Out of the Depths)

When the Chief Rabbi of Israel, Chief Rabbi Israel Meir Lau, told this story to Rebbe Menachem Schneerson, the spiritual leader of the Chabad movement of ultra-orthodox Jews, "pearls of tears" dropped from the Rebbe's eyes. Nothing more was said.

Viktor Frankl was a Viennese psychotherapist. The US offered him and his wife a visa at the war's beginning, but it didn't cover his elderly parents. The dilemma it provoked was resolved when his father showed him the fifth commandment – "Honor thy father and thy mother" – inscribed on a shard that survived the destruction of their synagogue. Viktor forfeited the visa. It wasn't long before the Nazis abducted his parents and young wife, murdering them during the three years Viktor spent in Auschwitz.

In prison, Viktor used his imprisonment to develop his theory of Logotherapy, the Greek for "meaning." Frankl believed that finding purpose or meaning in life was humanity's primary motivation. In *Man's Search for Meaning,* he proposes that freedom of choice is the "ultimate freedom." Even if we cannot change our circumstances, our freedom of choice allows us to change our attitude to our situation. Creative deeds or work, experience of someone or something, or our attitude to life, Frankl believed, were the three ways in which we can achieve meaning. Frankl thinking rests on three principles:

- *He who has a "why" to live for, can bear almost any "how"*: success and happiness, then, are the byproducts of always doing our best;
- *Love is the ultimate and highest goal to which man can aspire*: follow a cause greater than yourself; always seek to do good and be righteous in all you do;
- *When we are no longer able to change the situation, we are challenged to change ourselves*: Never apportion blame; take responsibility; look at life through the eyes of love.

None of these concepts are new. Tom Quinn, who wrote *The Reluctant Billionaire: The Tragic Life of Gerald Grosvenor, Sixth Duke of Westminster*, explained that many billionaires suffer from a sense of "pointlessness," particularly in the case of inherited wealth which does not flow from personal achievement. In *Eight Paths of Purpose*, Tuvia Teldon states:

The most advanced primates do not try to make life better for future generations. They all have the luxury of fulfilling their purpose by doing exactly what they are programmed to do, but they can't intentionally change or break through their limitations. They don't have to deal with the paradox of purpose. We alone have this amazing gift of purpose which makes each of us so unique in the universe, and we alone have to overcome the paradox of purpose by choosing to fulfil our purpose.

The ultimate meaning of life, then, is not something we know, but something that must be created and found by maintaining the highest standards. After all, we can't really explain what music or art or love is – we must find their meaning for ourselves. This is equally true of belief, faith and the existence of God. But fulfilling our purpose rarely comes without internal struggle. Yet our most formidable challenges offer the greatest potential for refinement and wisdom; they are designed to bring out our best. It follows that there are no problems, only solutions. We find greatness when doubts consume us, when all looks bleak. We are imbued with the emotional strength to stand after we stumble, to endure when the path is unendurable. We are endowed with the power to finish everything we start, the persistence to follow through, the determination to go the distance, and the tenacity to complete the most difficult of tasks. Activating these powers is a personal endeavor. We can't assume others' pain. We must learn to love ourselves. I often played *The Greatest Love of All* as my theme song, emphasizing the lyrics and what they stood for. In the end, living a life of love is its meaning and purpose.

Wouldn't it be lovely?

END

References

Deepak Chopra, The Seven Spiritual Laws of Success

Deepak Chopra, Life After Death

Deepak Chopra, Quantum Healing

Dan Millman, The Life you were born to live

Paul Coelho, The Alchemist

Elizabeth Brown, Living Successfully with Screwed up People

Terry Eagleton, The Meaning of Life

James Redfield, The Celestial Prophecy

Dalai Lama XIV, with Howard Culter

Rollo May, Mans' Search for Himself

Eckhart Tolle, A New Earth, Awakening Your Life

M. Scott Peck, The Road Less Travelled

Dr. Becky Liguori, Our Return to Oneness

Mitch Albom, Tuesday with Morrie

Hermann Hesse, Siddhartha

Marianne Williamson, A Course in Miracles

Edgar Cayce, The Power of Your Mind

Robert D. Hare, Without Conscience: Disturbing World Psychopaths Among Us

Morey Bernstein, The Search for Bridey Murphy

Dr. Wayne Dyer, Change Your Thoughts, Change Your Life

Sherwin Sherwin B.Nuland, How We Die

Stephen Covey, The 7 Habits of Highly Effective People

Berlinger, After Harm; Medical Error & Ethics of Forgiveness

Arthur Kurzwell, The Torah for Dummies

Valter Longo, The Longevity Diet

Rick Warren, The Purpose Driven Life

Dr. Jenna Macciochi, The Science of Staying Well

Jeremy Griffith, The End of the Human Condition

Dan Ariely, Predictably Irrational: hidden forces that shape our decisions

Norman Leberecht, Genius & Anxiety

Mendel Kalmenson, Positivity Bias

Martin Blaser, Missing Microbes

Atul Gewande, Being Mortal

Arthur Herman, The Cave and the Light: Plato versus Aristotle

C. Elliott. L. Smith, Anxiety and Depression Workbook for Dummies

Judith Beck, Cognitive Therapy for Challenging Problems

Othniel J Seiden, MD, Communing with the Dead, death needn't part you

Shanahan & Shanahan, Deep Nutrition ; Why Your Genes Need Traditional Food

Dr. J McGregor, The Empathy Trap Understanding Antisocial Personalities

Donna Eden, Energy Medicine: How to use your bodies Energy

Jonathan Haid, The Happiness Hypothesis: Putting Ancient Wisdom & Philosophy to the test of Modern Science

Yuval Harari, Homo Deus: A Brief History of Tomorrow

Michael Gregor, How not to Die

E. Yaverbaum, Leadership Secrets of the World's Most Successful CEOs

Yoram Hazony, The Philosophy of Hebrew Scripture

Charles Duhigg, The Power of Habit: Why We do What We Do

Anne Lamott, Help, Thanks, Wow, The Three Essential Prayers

Daniel Kahneman, Thinking Fast and Slow

Tim LaHaye, Why You Act the Way You Do

Chief Rabbi Israel Meir Lau, Out of the Depths

**PSYCHE
BOOKS**

PSYCHE BOOKS
PSYCHOLOGY

Psyche Books cover all aspects of psychology and matters relating to the head.

The study of the mind - interactions, behaviors, functions; developing and expanding our understanding of self.

Psychology: All forms, all disciplines including business, criminal, educational, sport. Therapies: clinical analysis, CBT, counselling, hypnosis, NLP, psychoanalysis, psychodrama, psychotherapy, role-play.

Archetypes, behavioral science, CAM therapies, experimental work, popular psychology, psychological studies, neuroscience. Including but not restricted to: Behavior, brain games, personality, mental health, mind coaching, nature of the mind, treatment strategies, unconscious mind.

If you have enjoyed this book, why not tell other readers by posting a review on your preferred book site.

The Chi of Change
How Hypnotherapy Can Help You Heal and Turn Your Life
Around - Regardless of Your Past
Peter Field
A ground breaking book that will change forever the way you
think about your feelings and emotions!
Paperback: 978-1-78279-351-9 ebook: 978-1-78279-350-2

Emotional Life
Managing Your Feelings to Make the Most of Your Precious Time
on Earth How to Gain Mastery Over Your Feelings
Doreen Davy
Emotional Life explains how we can harness our own emotional
power in order to live happier, healthier and more fulfilling lives.
Paperback: 978-1-78279-276-5 ebook: 978-1-78279-275-8

Creating Trance and Hypnosis Scripts
Gemma Bailey
A well-known hypnotherapist reveals her secret tips on how to
help others quit smoking, lose weight and beat the blues.
Paperback: 978-1-84694-197-9

Depression: Understanding the Black Dog
Stephanie June Sorrell
This accessible work addresses a universal health issue with a
toolbag yielding the ways depression manifests and insight into
the treatments available.
Paperback: 978-1-78279-165-2 ebook: 978-1-78279-174-4

Smashing Depression
Escaping the Prison and Finding a Life
Terence Watts
Depression is an insidious enemy, gradually eroding confidence
and willpower... but this book restores the spirit and strength to
fight back - and win!
Paperback: 978-1-78279-619-0 ebook: 978-1-78279-618-3

Why Men Like Straight Lines and Women Like Polka Dots
Gender and Visual Psychology
Gloria Moss
Discover how men and women perceive the world differently and
why they won't agree on the colour or shape of the sofa!
Paperback: 978-1-84694-857-2 ebook: 978-1-84694-708-7

Head versus Heart
Michael Hampson
The most important new material on the enneagram in thirty
years, Head Versus Heart questions how we engage with the world
around us.
Paperback: 978-1-90381-692-9

Mastering Your Self, Mastering Your World
Living by the Serenity Prayer
John William Reich
Mastery over the events of our life is key to our well-being; this
book explains how to achieve that mastery.
Paperback: 978-1-78279-727-2 ebook: 978-1-78279-726-5

The Secret Life of Love and Sex
Making Relationships Work and What to Do If They Don't
Terence Watts
Men and women think differently and 'work' differently - but they
don't know that! SO sometimes a white lie or a secret is a
good thing...
Paperback: 978-1-78279-464-6 ebook: 978-1-78279-463-9

Powerful Mind Through Self-Hypnosis
A Practical Guide to Complete Self-Mastery
Cathal O'Briain
Powerful Mind Through Self-Hypnosis is the definitive book, teaching
self-hypnosis as a pure and natural form of self-healing.
Paperback: 978-1-84694-298-3 ebook: 978-1-78099-761-2

Readers of ebooks can buy or view any of these bestsellers by
clicking on the live link in the title. Most titles are published in
paperback and as an ebook. Paperbacks are available in traditional
bookshops. Both print and ebook formats are available online.

Find more titles and sign up to our readers' newsletter at http://
www.johnhuntpublishing.com/mind-body-spirit. Follow us on
Facebook at https://www.facebook.com/OBooks and Twitter at
https://twitter.com/obooks.